An intriguing book this. burned and was burned b years of his ministry. The way will be a great help to If you're wise you'll learn i ____s and rejoice in his redemption (from himself).

MEZ MCCONNELL
Pastor, Niddrie Community Church and Director of 20schemes
Edinburgh, Scotland

Read this book and be encouraged that God uses your mistakes while making you wiser in the process. When you go through difficult times as a pastor or church planter, you can miss the lessons God has for you. Don't be that guy! Learn to flourish in the place God placed you. Learn how to prepare a banquet for those God calls you to love and lead. The lessons are humorous and insightful and encouraging to all of us who aspire to be servant leaders in our churches.

MARK GREEN
President, White Horse Inn
Escondido, California

Kyle McClellan has written the most unusual type of book about ministry: an honest one. Like Kent Hughes' marvelous *Liberating Ministry from the Success Syndrome*, this book tells the truth about failure, discouragement, and the necessity of making faithfulness the chief mark of one's life, marriage, and ministry. Kyle's honesty and helpfulness demonstrates the power of God's discipline and hope. Young ministers ought to read the book as a warning and an opportunity. Older ministers need to read the book as a call to humble mentoring of the next generation.

PAUL R HOUSE
Professor of Divinity
Beeson Divinity School of Samford University
Birmingham, Alabama

Many men dream of writing books about their ministry success. Few dream of recording their failures. With a humorous tone, a humble posture, and a pastor's heart, Kyle McClellan shares where he got punched in the mouth so we'd know when to duck. This is an invaluable book to a generation of emerging pastors being called to shepherd the local church. The only thing I don't appreciate about *Mea Culpa* is that McClellan didn't write it 10 years ago.

GAVIN JOHNSON
Lead Pastor, City Light Church
Omaha, Nebraska

Mea Culpa is not what you expect. What you expect is a weak attempt to admit failures, a glossing over of personal fault, opacity instead of transparency, and excuses rather than reality. *Mea Culpa* delivers a raw view of truth and through that truth, a pathway to contentment, peace and forgiveness through the power of God. I've known Kyle for some time now, and he has once again delivered what I would expect from him – unvarnished insight that will meet you where you really live. There is meat in every page – something I find missing in most evangelical books today. Read it and then live it.

ED WEAVER
CEO, T4Global
Dallas, Texas

The late Jack Miller used to say, "Cheer up! You are worse off than you think!" It was his way of telling people that we are worse-off sinners met by a most-amazing grace. Strikingly, though we pastors preach this message, we are often the last ones to believe it. Kyle McClellan has learned the lessons of grace deeply, painfully, and profoundly.

How do I know? Turn the pages of *Mea Culpa* and find out. Only someone who has learned that he is loved by a God of steadfast, covenant love can tell the truth about himself, his ministry, and his hope that God can use sinners like us. Learn from Kyle's missteps, but even more, embrace the God of grace to whom he gives testimony.

SEAN MICHAEL LUCAS
Senior Minister, The First Presbyterian Church
Associate Professor of Church History
Reformed Theological Seminary/Jackson
Hattiesburg, Mississippi

Brace yourself for some uncomfortable levels of honesty as Kyle McClellan lifts the lid on some of the peculiar struggles of pastoral ministry. This book feels like a long chat in the car with engine turned off. Lessons long in the learning are shared with wit and wisdom, self-deprecation and humility. You will wince at Kyle's mistakes, grow wiser through his insights, and find fresh hope that a pastor can be used by God despite all of his faults and foibles.

COLIN ADAMS
Pastor, Ballymoney Baptist Church
Ballymoney, Northern Ireland

Mea Culpa

Learning from Mistakes
in the Ministry

KYLE MCCLELLAN

Kyle McClellan is the founding pastor of Grace Church (PCA) in his hometown of Fremont, Nebraska. Kyle holds degrees from Taylor University, The Southern Baptist Theological Seminary and may someday finish his D.Min. at Beeson Divinity School. He is an occasional contributor to Practical Shepherding, an organization committed to equipping pastors in practical matters of pastoral ministry. Kyle and his wife Amy have two children: Gabrielle and Nathaniel. *Mea Culpa* is a joint publication with *Practical Shepherding.*

Copyright © Kyle McClellan 2015

paperback ISBN 978-1-78191-529-5
epub ISBN 978-1-78191-530-1
Mobi ISBN 978-1-78191-531-8
Published in 2015 by Christian Focus Publications

Christian Focus Publications,
Geanies House,
Fearn, Tain, Ross-shire,
IV20 1TW, Great Britain.
www.christianfocus.com

Practical Shepherding, Inc
P.O. Box 21806
Louisville, KY 40221
U.S.A.
www.practicalshepherding.com

Cover design by Dufi-Art

Printed and bound by
Bell and Bain, Glasgow

MIX
Paper from
responsible sources
FSC® C007785

CONTENTS

FOREWORD 11

INTRODUCTION 15

LESSON ONE
Why a big theological melon will not overcome
    a sinful, selfish heart.. 25

LESSON TWO
What Wendell Berry can teach us about place 33

LESSON THREE
The myth of prophetic fits.. 45

LESSON FOUR
Jesus wants me to squat, bench and deadlift............... 59

LESSON FIVE
Find your preaching voice – not someone else's 71

LESSON SIX
Live on the knife-edge of authenticity and godliness...... 85

LESSON SEVEN
Try not to be a train wreck as a husband and father .. 93

ENDING ON A GOOD NOTE
Two for the road...105

CONCLUSION.. 111

ACKNOWLEDGEMENTS...113

DEDICATION

When I harbored dreams of an academic life,
I told myself my first book would be dedicated
to my wife. However, we both agree that this is
more fitting:

for Jodi and Eric Blick

May the gospel quiet your grief.

FOREWORD

There is a disturbing trend among modern evangelical churches today—short pastorates. Depending upon whom you asked, the average stay for a pastor in a church today is about two to three years. These short stints are the result of many factors. Pastors get easily discouraged when their expectations don't get met, and they leave. Churches with unhealthy, dysfunctional habits sometimes chew up their pastors and spit them out. Larger churches with more money and prestige woo pastors away, and each church becomes a stepping stone to the next bigger and better place. Some pastors go into their first church with guns blazing and get themselves fired in the first year. The rigors of pastoral ministry wear on some pastors to the point of burnout, which then causes a pastor to leave his church and even ministry altogether. Pastors are now dropping out in record numbers and there appears to be no sign this will subside.

The more I work with pastors all around the world, the more I am finding that those who have terrible experiences pastoring a church often leave the ministry altogether. The hurt and pain is just too much. Some might try again, thinking they just landed in a bad church, but if the next one goes bad as well, most are done for good with the ministry. Regardless of all the efforts and sacrifices a man makes to be educated and trained for pastoral ministry, that training cannot trump the wounds that remain. Like any reasonable man, he goes on to do something else.

Such is not the case for my dear friend, Kyle McClellan, who wrote this book. Kyle experienced many of the things listed above. He has gone into a church with guns blazing and was quickly fired. He has experienced the disappointment of unmet expectations and left because of it. He has pastored a destructive church that chewed him up and spat him out. He has felt the pull of the bigger and better church trying to woo him away. He has faced the burnout and fatigue that many pastors experience that causes them to bail. Some of you might be asking, "So, what makes Kyle unique to these experiences?" Kyle has kept serving in pastoral ministry when most would have quit long ago. Why is this?

Some might say Kyle is just a glutton for punishment. That might be true to some extent (as he would admit). But what I observed as I watched him endure so many of these painful experiences was a man God was molding and shaping through them. God was at work teaching him. God was at work humbling a prideful heart. God was at work displaying the resolve to press on that every man truly called of God to be a shepherd to his people possesses. God has brought Kyle through the fires of adversity and made him a sweet, humble, transparent, and broken man that now possesses wisdom far beyond his years.

That wisdom is what you will find in this book and why I strongly commend this book and man to you. Kyle shares some of the lessons he learned in those painful years with a raw transparency that is refreshing and engaging to read. When I asked Kyle to write this book, he hesitantly agreed. After all, who wants to write a book about all the mistakes we make? Neither did Kyle, but I had a hunch that this book would uniquely serve pastors who are struggling in ways no resource I know of can. After reading the finished product, I believe you hold in your hand that gem. It is the reason I am convinced Kyle's pastoral ministry is now flourishing.

Read this book. Learn from him. Receive these essential lessons from a wise, broken man who has lived it, possesses the scars from it, owns the T-shirt, and yet by the grace of God still stands. May God use these lessons and Kyle's example to make you a faithful shepherd of God's people until the Chief Shepherd returns.

Brian Croft
Pastor, Auburndale Baptist Church
Founder, Practical Shepherding
March 2014

INTRODUCTION

My friend Brian Croft likes pastors – I mean he **really** likes them. All of them. Me? Not so much. Oh, I like some of them just fine. But the ones who want to tell you how to dress and how to be a relevant communicator, so that you can build your own marketable kingdom? Those guys make me want to call down the Thunder of Hulkamania, drop the people's elbow, and ask them if they can smell what the Rock is cooking[1]. Not Brian Croft. Brian likes those pastors too. He doesn't agree with them, but he wants to serve them well. Brian's blog *Practical Shepherding* is proof positive of his love and

---

1   I grew up watching the WWF like it was my job. Pro wrestling really is the theater of the absurd. The bombast of Hulk Hogan and The Rock strike me as an appropriate response to guys who want to reduce gospel ministry to a particular set of relevant techniques.

concern for those who labor as pastors. And so, my buddy Croft is to blame for this book.

I never wanted to be a pastor, or a writer. But God called me to the first, and Brian thinks the lessons I've learned would be helpful to pastors. Since, as we've already determined, Brian likes and wants to serve pastors, I find myself writing.

To that end, my prayer is that the book you're holding would be helpful to pastors. All I can share with you is my story, and the lessons I've learned. As we'll discuss later, one of the lessons I've learned is that a pastor has to be authentic. I think most pastors are tired of flim-flammery, and just want somebody to say what needs to be said. There is an art to being plain-spoken, and here in Nebraska we value that art highly.

I'm a PCA (Presbyterian Church in America) church planter living and ministering in my hometown of Fremont, Nebraska. There's nothing particularly earth-shattering about that, I know – but here's the rub: if you had told me ten years ago that this would be the case, I would have laughed at you, cussed at you, punched you – or some combination of all three. Why? Well, probably because I would have told you that I was either not gifted for it, theologically opposed to it, or would never, ever, ever in a million years think of going back to The 'Mont[2].

Not Gifted for It
I would have told you, ten years ago, that I was a pastor/theologian. Preaching and teaching were

---

2   Short for Fremont

my primary gifts – not the kind of glad-handed evangelism I thought was a part of church planting. I mocked, with great scorn and contempt, the guys who were a part of the Billy Graham School of Missions, Evangelism, and Church Growth at Southern Seminary.[3] "Maybe, when they grow up, they'll put their big boy pants on and read some books without pictures in them." I mean, who actually thinks you can plant a church around Word, prayer and sacrament? Thanks but no thanks.

Theologically Opposed to the PCA

As an undergraduate Bible major at Taylor University, I read John Piper's *Desiring God*. It was my first introduction to the idea that God is sovereign in salvation. Reading that book carpet-bombed any theological system I thought I had growing up in a revivalistic, largely Arminian, evangelical tradition. I entered Southern Seminary as a "Piper Calvinist" and grew in my love and understanding for the sovereignty of God – especially as it related to the salvation of sinners. While I was certainly sympathetic to Reformed/Presbyterian soteriology, well, they baptized babies – didn't they? Having grown up in a low church tradition that did not place particular value on the ordinances, I grew in my understanding of their value for local church life while in seminary. But it still seemed to me that the Presbyterians had the wrong end of the stick when it came to baptism. Again, thanks but no thanks.

---

3 While I was at SBTS, there was a healthy spirit of competition between the School of Theology and the Graham School (think inter-house competition at Hogwarts). I hear this is still the case.

Never Going Back

> "The plains leave an indelible mark upon one's soul – both for good and for ill." – Willa Cather

The joke in high school was: Fremont is a great place to be *from*, but I wouldn't want to live there. Athletics was my ticket out of my hometown, and while I enjoyed coming back to visit my parents, I had felt the ill mark of the plains upon my soul. Thanks, but "wild horses and nickel beer" couldn't drag me back.

How Do I Get There From Here?
So, with three strikes, how did I get here? First, through my mistakes – I plowed quite a bit of ministerial ground with my chin. Second, to quote my grandparents: "The Lord God Almighty overruled our (my) dumbness."[4] While the second factor certainly trumps the first, my mistakes are much easier to identify, discuss, and learn from, and these are the basis for what follows. The second is cause for doxology, but not so good for analyzing – that is for another book and another time.

Let me put it another way: from 1996-2006 I pastored four different churches. The first (while in seminary) was from November 1996-1999. The second: 1999-2000. The third: 2000-2003. Finally, the anchor leg went from 2003-2006. Only one of

---

4   While in their 60s, my maternal grandparents were mugged in their driveway. My grandfather was a WWII Navy vet, and tried to fight the two guys off. One of them had a gun, and grandpa was shot in the hip. When interviewed by the *Omaha World Herald* afterwards, Grandpa gave testimony to his own stupidity <u>and</u> God's goodness.

those congregations was sad to see me go. Two of them ended with me resigning and pitching a fit on my way out the door. The remaining church found the deacons asking me to leave, and I had the good sense to ask for some time to find a new place of ministry. Not a great start for a guy who had been told he was a "five-talent minister" (referencing the Parable of the Talents in Matthew 25) and was a Preaching Award Winner while in seminary.

Mea Culpa

There's no use denying that there are unhealthy churches out there, or that some churches would be of highest use to the Kingdom if they decided to close their doors. That, however, is beyond the scope of my concern here. My concern is that we learn from our mistakes, quit blaming others for *everything*, and move forward in a way that demonstrates God's grace to His people. Take the attitude of an athlete watching game tape: I messed up. *Mea culpa.* In response to my mistake, I'll learn, take steps to correct it, and (by God's grace) do better next time.

Wendell Berry is one of my favorite authors. This makes sense given that the first church I pastored was in Henry County, Kentucky (where Berry lives) and I currently labor in an agrarian context (a common Berry theme). My favorite Berry character is Burley Coulter. One of Burley's oft-quoted phrases is, "I never learned nothing 'till I had to."

In that regard, I am Burley Coulter.

I suspect that some of you are as well. But here

is what my friend Croft has learned: most guys have a couple of tough go-rounds with churches, and then leave the ministry altogether. They are mad, bitter, damaged, and, in their minds, totally blameless. There's the rub: it would be one thing if we were perfect in our pastoral ministries. We're not. So, let's pray together that God will use the mistakes I've already made as a lesson, and a warning. Let's pray that for the sake of the church and the glory of God, we would quit making some of the same mistakes.

You may have picked up this book because the title intrigued you: *Mea Culpa*. Much of the hardship I've endured in ministry has been my own doing. This hardship was rooted in mistakes I made, stupidity that I embraced, sin I needed to confess (but didn't). It's easy to blame the idiot board of deacons, or the church diva whose tongue really is "a restless evil, full of deadly poison" (James 2:8) and yet she somehow gets a free pass? It's much harder to look in the mirror and *mea culpa*. I think it's one of the reasons pastors HATE to be evaluated. We don't want others pointing out growth areas, or just the fact that we are redeemed sinners who royally mess up on a regular basis. My late friend and golfing buddy Floyd Goff used to put it this way (usually following a 3-putt bogey), "Preacher, I believe we're pooping in our own mess kit."

Having played and coached college athletics, I realize the importance of looking at the tape. Game tape does not lie. You may think you made an All-American type play, only to see that the opposite is true. A player may plead to their excellence of execution on the sideline following a boneheaded play – but the tape will tell the truth. This book is my tape. Read it and laugh, if you like. However, please don't read it and then do the same stupid stuff I've done. Read and learn. I've enough scars on my back for both of us. The church of Jesus Christ deserves better.

Paul David Tripp makes this point much more eloquently than I can. He reminds us, "I know pastors not only face trouble but also can be all too skilled at troubling their own trouble."[5] Until we understand this and are willing to take an honest look at our short-comings and failures, I fear we are doomed to find ourselves in a painful cycle.

Picking

Providentially, it took three months of walking 20+ miles a day picking books at the Amazon warehouse and the wise counsel of a friend to learn this. After I resigned, I still had a wife, two kids, and a mortgage. The church gave me three months' severance – so I had to find a job. What did my big, bad M.Div. and "five-talent skills" get me? They got me a job working 10-hour shifts at Amazon. Jesus and I had some stuff to straighten out. I thought most of it was His – but it turns out I was wrong. I would walk (did I mention it was 20+ miles a day?), pick books, and rage inwardly to the One who called me to ministry. It took every day of the

---

5   Paul David Tripp, *Dangerous Calling.* (Crossway, Wheaton, IL: 2012). p. 29.

three months for me to finally shut up and listen.

At the same time, a wise and experienced pastor friend of mine encouraged me to find an older pastor (not in my denomination) and try to get the color and number of the bus that had just run over me. John Sartelle did not know me from Adam, but he graciously gave of his time and counsel. We met every week for a year. John listened to me vent and asked questions. The good folks at Tates Creek Presbyterian Church bestowed love and grace to our damaged[6] and gun-shy family. The Lord God Almighty was overruling my dumbness. I was finally at a place where the honest assessment of my own mistakes could now begin.

So what did I learn? What mistakes did I iden-tify? They are legion, but I've generally clumped them into seven categories. Chapter one addresses what Paul Tripp covers much more thoughtfully in his book *Dangerous Calling*: a big, theological mel-on[7] will not overcome a sinful, selfish heart when you're a pastor. Chapter two addresses a Wendell Berry-type theme: place. Chapter three deals with the myth of prophetic fits and their value for min-istry. Chapter four addresses the need for balance in our lives. Chapter five urges us to find our voice in the pulpit. Chapter six challenges us to live

---

6   My wife Amy is amazing. She never once suggested we chuck the church thing and move on. Instead, she affirmed my calling and God's goodness to us – channeling her inner Barbara Hughes (if you've not read Kent & Barbara Hughes, *Liberating Ministry from the Success Syndrome*, shame on you).

7   I use the term "melon" here in its colloquial sense of "head" or "brain."

on the knife-edge of authenticity and godliness. Chapter seven painfully shares lessons learned from being a train wreck as a husband and father, and finally, I offer some concluding thoughts "for the road."

Monday is a day of reckoning for college football players. It's the day you watch the game film from the preceding Saturday. Our Defensive Coordinator at Taylor University was a man named John Moses. I loved John. He had a winsome way of pointing out how you had completely messed up on a particular play. Coach Moses would say things like, "You know Mac, for being a college man and a good football player, that was dumb. I know you know better – tell me what you should have done." Sometimes, an opponent just physically overpowered you. John would then say, "I love how quickly you pursued to the ball after being whipped. How about we not get whipped, or we'll find somebody else?" Every failure was a teaching moment, and a chance for further motivation.

In your mind's eye, pretend you've just sat down on the second floor of the Field House. You sit on the defensive side of the room, next to Eric "He-Man" Hehman and Scott "Tito" Sanchez. The lights go off. The D-Line coach, Bud Badger, sits next to the defensive linemen, and Coach Moses controls the tape. Class is in session. You can run, but you can't hide. The tape will find you.

That's where we find ourselves now. I'm going to "run the tape" on my own life, and you might just find that you recognize some or all of your own pastoral moves on the screen in front of us. Let's look at these together to see if we can't find a way to improve...

Why a big theological melon will not overcome a sinful, selfish heart

My Dumbness

I've had the privilege of going to good schools. Not Ivy League good, but *"U.S. News and World Report* top schools" good. To be honest, my entrance into Taylor University had nothing to do with my academic prowess. I got in because I could play football. While at Taylor, I met Paul House. Paul took an athlete with an aversion to academics and introduced him to the life of the mind. At Paul's suggestion, I did my M.Div. at the Southern Baptist Theological Seminary (SBTS). I enjoyed the work, and I enjoyed the camaraderie at SBTS in the mid to late 1990s. To top it all off, I met my wife Amy while at Southern, so I did more than OK.

Now, if you know nothing of Southern's story, a bit of background would be helpful. The Southern

Baptist Theological Seminary (SBTS) is the flagship of the six denominational seminaries operated by the Southern Baptist Convention. Prior to 1993, SBTS was steeped in moderate or liberal theology (depending on your perspective). J, E, D, and P were running amuck, skipping hand in hand with Deutero-Isaiah across the Josephus Bowl on campus. SBTS underwent a seismic theological shift to the right when R. Albert Mohler was hired in 1993 as a thirty-three-year old President. I got on campus a semester after Dr. Mohler arrived. The theological battles that followed were epic – so much so that a documentary was made by the son of a student and aired on PBS. My undergraduate work was in Bible, and the faculty at Taylor made sure we knew both sides of the coin theologically. I took great pride in the fact that I could hold my own academically in the midst of such upheaval. There were sit-ins, votes of no confidence, and my friend Jimmy Scroggins and I were asked to leave class more than once for giving voice to an evangelical viewpoint.

That's where the trouble began.

I did not grow up Southern Baptist. I was more than willing, however, to put myself smack dab in the middle of a good scrum. It was a fight worth having – orthodoxy is always worth defending – but engaging in the fight left me proud. And goodness knows, the last thing I needed was something else to be cocky about. I came to welcome the conflict, to welcome the fact that I could walk into a classroom with both guns blazing. I loved the turmoil. One friend would later refer to me as a "theological bouncer." God calls me to shepherd His people, and I'm the bouncer? You can see where this is headed. The purpose of theological education is to prepare you to serve the church, not to give you a theological arsenal to unleash upon unsuspecting congregants.

Southern Seminary is not, however, alone in this issue. What made Southern unique is that the theological conflicts were not about minutia, but about the doctrine of Scripture. There is a broader problem in most Western seminaries: theological education becomes about finding your theological niche. Are you an infralapsarian or a supralapsarian? Do you grasp the eschatological ramifications of the *parousia*? What's worse, we think that our hissy fits about minutia should somehow transform people's lives. Again, Paul Tripp presents us with great insight:

> I personally experienced what can happen when the gospel of Jesus Christ gets reduced to a series of theological ideas coupled with all the skills necessary to access those ideas. Bad things happen when maturity is more defined by knowing than it is by being. Danger is afloat when you come to love the ideas more than the God whom they represent and the people they are meant to free.[1]

I feel really bad for the good folks of the Cornerstone Baptist Church in Elgin, Texas. Most of them are really good people. They want to serve and honor the Lord. They got a hot-shot, preaching-award-winning

---

1   *Dangerous Calling*, p. 42.

dude with a cute wife right out of seminary. I could bring the theological thunder with the best of them. I was twenty-nine, had been married for four years, and did not have a single clue. Heaven help them.

What they needed was a pastor. They needed a shepherd. They needed a guy whose walk with Jesus was the life-blood of his ministry. Sadly, that's not what they got. They got a guy whose sermons sounded more like theological lectures than sermons. The basics of a confessional, Calvinistic, baptistic faith were hammered home to them. Three times a week, for forty-five minutes a pop, they were subjected to my cluelessness.

I can look back and tell you that part of the problem I faced in that first pastorate was making the move from the academy to the local church. In the academy, a question is often a call to arms. It's a chance to cross swords and engage in intellectual pugilism. I loved it (still do).[2] However, more often than not, when normal people ask a question, it's because they are genuinely struggling with whatever they asked. Now, there are always a few goofball outliers – but generally, questions are asked in good faith. So, when those questions presented an opportunity for me to *love* the people of God, I *lectured* them instead.

---

2   I love 99 per cent of Jim Belcher's *Deep Church* (Downer's Grove, IL: IVP, 2009). However, his assessment that Carl F.H. Henry's epistemology is tied too closely to the rationalism of the enlightenment is, in my estimation, a misreading of Henry (48). I rejoice in my friend Gregory Alan (Thunder) Thornbury's *Recovering Classic Evangelicalism* (Wheaton, IL: Crossway, 2013). Greg has given a Bane-type knee to the spine to those who hold Belcher's view.

Coming from Southern just made it worse. Classes in the early days at SBTS were a Battle Royale: the last man standing was declared the winner. Ask me a question and you got both guns. Challenge me and I'll crush you. Somehow, the dichotomy of defending the faith while acting like a jerk never came home to me.

Part of this tension can certainly be traced to the fact that I hold to Calvinist soteriology while serving in a denomination (Southern Baptist Convention) that was/is torn over that issue. I knew of guys getting fired for being Calvinists. It felt like a "guns up" issue. Having to defend, on a regular basis, the foundational truths by which sinful humans are reconciled to a holy, loving God gets wearisome. Still, you can win an argument, but lose the person. I got pretty good at that.

However, the real reason for my argumentative responses was much more simple and painful. I responded this way because I am an arrogant sinner. I perceive questions as a challenge to my "pastoral authority" because I am arrogant. I'll try to bury you because I really am a sinner. Since I'm not secure in the gospel, I'm trying to validate my ministry by my own strength and intellect. It's both a me *project*, and a me *problem*. It is an area for growth, and a sin issue that needs to be confessed.

How the Gospel Overrules My Dumbness
Preaching systematically through books of the Bible has saved my bacon on numerous occasions. I marvel at what God does through His Word – not

only in the life of the congregation, but in my life as well. The reinstatement of Peter in John 21:15-19 is a passage I revisit on a regular basis. Let me play the role of redactor and rewrite the passage as I lived it out in my early years of ministry:

> Jesus: *Kyle, son of Dave, are you more gifted than these?*
>
> Kyle: *Yes, Lord; you know I'm a "five-talent" minister.*
>
> Jesus: *Display your giftedness so that all can see it.*
>
> Jesus: *Kyle, son of Dave, are you theologically well-read and orthodox?*
>
> Kyle: *Yes, Lord; you know I'd argue theology with anyone.*
>
> Jesus: *Make sure these intellectual slackers and liberals are shown the error of their ways.*
>
> Jesus: *Kyle, son of Dave, are you called to preach?*
>
> Kyle: *Lord, you know everything; you know you've called me to preach.*
>
> Jesus: *Bring the thunder then!*

Thankfully, that's not how the passage unfolds. Instead, Jesus asks Peter three times if he loves Him. He does not enquire as to his giftedness, his orthodoxy, or his sense of calling. At the root of ministry that will not create havoc in the hearts of congregation and minister is this one thing: love for Jesus. It is in the context of loving Jesus that Peter is given his marching orders: feed/tend the flock of Christ. Calling/preparation/giftedness are not the issues here. Love for Jesus is.

Now, some uber-theological Poindexter or super nerdy guy may ask, "So – are you saying these things are not important? That calling, theological orthodoxy, sound preparation, and giftedness make no difference?" Of course they do! However, ministry must be an act of obedience to the one my soul loves more than anyone or anything else. If not, I will make a hash of what I've been called/prepared/gifted by God to do. It will be about me, and not about the Savior. My love of me will trump my love of Jesus every time. In time I realized, quite painfully, that my efforts in ministry were not an expression of my love for Christ. As I've thought further about this, I don't think I was trying to *earn* Christ's love by my work – but the work certainly was not an expression of love for my Savior.

This realization was only half the story, however. Once I realized the error of my ways, there remained the problem of addressing the issue. How do we cultivate this love for Christ?

In the introduction to his book, *Practical Religion*, J. C. Ryle says the following: "After forty years of Bible-reading and praying, meditation and theological study, I find myself clinging more than ever to 'Evangelical' religion, and more than ever satisfied with it. It wears well: it stands the fire." [3]

Nothing flashy: read the Book (Bible reading). Talk to Him (prayer). Think about Him (meditation). Think about Him in a historically informed and logically consistent way (theological study). Approach my love for Jesus in much the same way I cultivate my love for my wife.

I've also realized that, much like my marriage and love for Amy, growing in my love for Jesus via

---

3   J.C. Ryle, *Practical Religion* (Carlisle, PA: The Banner of Truth, 1998), vi-vii.

these means of grace is a lifelong endeavor. I enjoy hearing older ministers talk of the ways Christ has displayed His faithfulness to them. It's not all, "Back in my day ..." lamentations. Like a good marriage, they've labored in this love relationship for a number of years, and the fruit of that love is evident. I ought to be able to speak and write about this in a much fuller and deeper way ten years from now than I can today.

What about you? Are you cultivating your ability to beat the foolishness out of any who dare defy your intellectual or theological prowess?[4] Or, are you using these means of grace, not to show you're the smartest kid in the class, but as a means to grow in your love for the Savior? For the sake of your soul, and the souls of those in your care, I pray it's the latter.

---

4   Confession time: I've watched *South Park* (twice, in fact). Some dudes come off sounding like Cartman, "Respect my authority!" Don't be that guy.

What Wendell Berry can teach us about place

I love where I live. I love the fact that I can walk to work – past the old middle school building where I spent my freshman year, through John C. Fremont Park, past the old power plant (now converted into wicked cool loft apartments). It's a great ten-minute walk, even on those days it's so cold that Beowulf and the crew would be looking for their long johns. I love the fact that I can walk down the street and say hello to Vince at *The Yankee Peddler* as I go to see Ginger at *The Blue Bottle* for my morning mocha. While I'm there, I can say hello to folks I recognize, many of whom I've known for thirty years. Everywhere I go here in Fremont, I know and am known. In short, this is the place of my belonging. The problem was, for quite a while I did not know I belonged here, largely because I did not want to belong here. In fact, I wanted nothing more than to put "here" in the rear-view mirror as quickly as possible.

I am a recovering gnostic. I don't deny the humanity of Jesus, so I'm not a gnostic in a Christological sense. I have, however, denied the importance of the actual setting in which God does His redemptive work in each of our lives. We don't live in "Anywhere" or "Somewhere." We all live and work and love and sin and struggle in a particular place. For too long in ministry, I devalued place.

Now please understand, I did not set out to live a crummy gnostic life. And I'm not particularly sure when gnosticism snuck into my soul. I do know, however, that once it was there it took some doing to get rid of it. Thankfully, I had help. A writer from Kentucky made sure the last vestiges of gnosticism were driven from my soul like Legion into a herd of swine. I have come to understand that one must love the gospel, the people you serve, and the place in which you live and work and minister.

How Did I Get Here?
As I look back, my family has always had a rather indifferent relationship to place. We were firmly rooted in Nebraska, but my folks both hailed from Omaha, and we lived in the Sandhills. Atkinson, Nebraska was two-and-a-half hours from the nearest McDonald's. The village of Atkinson is rural and remote, even by rural and remote standards. My dad was a teacher and high school coach, so even while we lived in and were shaped by that place, we

weren't "from there." Our presence in Atkinson was purely because of my father's vocational obligation to that place. We were not natives of the Sandhills. So, our family made frequent trips to Omaha, largely because that's where both sets of grandparents lived. Omaha felt like home, but it really wasn't.

We moved to Fremont right before my freshman year in high school. It was a hard transition. Fremont was a larger town (though not big by any standard), and I was used to my place in the social order of our smaller community. I struggled socially and academically, though not athletically. Football was my refuge, and I must admit, my god. False gods are ripped from our hands begrudgingly and painfully. My story is not unique in that regard. Much of my high school years were misspent chasing after my false god and all that accompanied it. It was not a great time in my life.

When the time came to look for colleges, I harbored an interesting stipulation: it had to be far away from Fremont. My two finalists, Wheaton College and Taylor University, shared three attributes: they were good academic institutions, they were serious about football, and they were at least eight hours away from Fremont. To say that Taylor won out because it was farther away is an overstatement, but not by much. Ironically, it was Taylor's likeness to the place I was trying hard to get away from that swayed me. Being a kid from Nebraska, Wheaton felt like downtown Chicago. Taylor, however, is literally in the middle of a cornfield. Game over.

Most of the students at Taylor were not from Upland, Indiana. There were a few faculty kids, and some folks from the surrounding area, but for the most part the student body was like me. We were all from somewhere else headed to wherever our college degree would make it possible for us to go after we graduated. College is not a great place for budding gnostics. There's too much theoretical knowledge and too many hypotheticals. We presume that "Anywhere, U.S.A." actually exists – even as we sit in our Michigan or Ohio State sweatshirts.

Are You a Yankee?

Deciding to go to Southern Seminary was akin to deciding to go to the moon to pursue a seminary education. This was an entirely new place and culture. I knew it within the first hours I spent on Southern's campus.

I got into Louisville late on a Saturday night. Upon arrival, I went to the residence director's apartment. The residence directors at Sampey Hall were a young couple from Georgia, who had just welcomed their first child into their lives. When I introduced myself to the husband as the wife sat on the couch with the newborn, she began to laugh. The conversation then went like this:

> He: (with a thick Georgia accent) What are you laughing at?
> She: (with a thicker accent): Well, God love him, he talks funny!

Not wanting to be rude and wanting desperately to get my key so that I could get my car unloaded and get settled in, I let the whole thing go. But I walked away wishing I had watched more episodes of the Andy Griffith Show in college. That, however, was just the beginning. My next-door neighbor was from Toccoa, Georgia. He had also played football in college, so I was hopeful this could be a good friendship (it was, and remains so). Upon our initial meeting, he looked me dead in the eye and asked a question with "blood earnestness": "So, Kylie, are you a Yankee?"

At this point, I was tired from the twelve-hour drive and unloading. I had absolutely no idea what to say. It was a question I had never been asked before. One of my college roommates hailed from Birmingham, Alabama. Slick had never accused or even asked if I was a Yankee. I had never exhibited Yankee-type behavior. This was a strange new world I had entered, and I was not entirely sure I liked it.

It got worse.
In my mind, Kentucky is the South, and Louisville is a part of Kentucky. Turns out I was wrong on both accounts. Kentucky is not the South; it is a part of Appalachia, and therefore a cousin to West Virginia. Not the South, but also not the North. President Lincoln moved into Kentucky after the Commonwealth made it clear that it wanted to join the Confederacy during the American Civil War. Lincoln's declaration of martial law stopped this. Not South, but not North.

As to Louisville, I foolishly thought it was a part of Kentucky. After all, my letters (people still sent mail of the non-electronic variety in those days) had a Kentucky address. My license plate was now blue and white and said KENTUCKY in big letters. But nope, not according to my classmates who hailed from other parts of Kentucky. Louisville is an entity all to itself. I should have known this, seeing as we have a similar situation here in Nebraska. Omaha is not really Nebraska: it's Omaha. Lincoln is everyone's second hometown, but Omaha is neither fish nor fowl. It's a world unto itself. My gnostic tendencies had found the perfect place to grow and flourish.

Eventually, I married a lovely girl from Kentucky and came to love Louisville. It is a beautiful city, and I am grateful that our annual trips back to see family allow Amy and me to introduce our kids to a place we love. Still, I wasn't from there, and didn't feel I belonged there. Hope, however, was on the way. A farmer from up Interstate 71, living, writing and farming in Port Royal, Kentucky, was about to come onto my radar screen. Too bad it took me ten years to take to heart what he was teaching me! It would get worse before it got better.

A Professional Gnostic

Our first church right out of seminary was in Elgin, Texas. After being there about six weeks, Amy and I realized we were not in Kentucky anymore. Texans are serious about being Texans. We joked that we should have been appointed by the International Mission Board to accept a pastoral call in Texas. The food was great, but we never really got used to the place. If our daughter Gabrielle had not been born in Austin, we could probably convince ourselves that we never sojourned in that far country. It was a very hard eighteen months of ministry, and I can look back and realize that my gnostic thinking regarding place contributed greatly to the difficulty. Texas was a new and strange place, and place matters.

Sadly, my default setting was that there was something wrong with that place. Not with me, or with my gnostic soul, or with my understanding and appreciation of that place. No, the fault was with the place – or so I thought.

I'd seen it happen from the other side as well: my youth pastor in high school was a Chicago native. He had the stereotypical Chicago accent and attitude. He hated Fremont; referring to the place as "jacked up." After three brutal years here, he and his wife moved on to Ohio. When I told him we were returning to Fremont to plant Grace, his response to me was telling: "Geez Kylie, that joint is jacked up. You sure you wanna do that?" Twenty years later and he still struggles with this place.

Enter Wendell Berry
My friends Sean Lucas and Richard Bailey first introduced me to the writings of Wendell Berry while I was in seminary. I met him on a couple of occasions: he lived in Henry County, Kentucky, and the first church I pastored was in rural Henry County. We met at an associational meeting,

and he came to Orville Baptist to hear me preach a couple of times. I fear he was coming to see if the "preacher boys" from Southern were as bad as he remembered. Indeed, I was.

The gospel is to be lived out in particular places. It is not an abstract philosophical concept. It calls us to love God and love neighbor. Not our neighbor in theory, but actual people. The gospel calls us into community, and not a community of our choosing. My gnostic soul had removed the gospel from particular places. I viewed the gospel as an astonishing, mind-blowing series of theological propositions. I did not preach it as a story that comes to us in our particular place. I do now, but not then.

I owe Wendell Berry a debt I can never repay. If it were not for Wendell Berry, I would have agreed with my youth pastor. I would have left Fremont never to return. In a strange way, the novels of Wendell Berry made it intellectually respectable for me to return to my hometown. Reading the exploits of Ptolemy and Minnie Proudfoot, Burley Coulter and the Catlett clan, impressed upon me the beauty of local economies. In whatever place God has put you, you are a part of the "local membership." As Burley Coulter sermonizes, "It ain't a matter of who's in and who's not. No beloved, it's a matter of who knows it and who don't." Loving the gospel is one thing, loving the people you serve is another, but you really must learn to love the place you minister as well. Not for what it could become, or what it was. You must come to love it for what it is. The gospel is not lived out in some disembodied way; our presence as Jesus-followers is an incarnational intrusion in a specific place. We are not gnostics.

Going to Africa to Love Nebraska

I re-entered ministry by serving with an orality-based missions organization in Lexington, Kentucky. From 2007-2010 I was responsible for creating the content used in Africa by T4 Global, an organization that provides messages of hope and help to the poorest and hardest-to-reach communities through oral culture. The three years I spent with T4 Global were invaluable for helping me overcome my gnosticism. Our work was focused and specific. It was tied to a tribal language group, and therefore a place. Some tribal groups, such as the Fulani in Africa, are nomadic. Most, however, are semi-nomadic herdsman, and therefore do have a specific place on this earth. Their story is tied to place. Their tribe has a place of belonging.

Any day that starts in Kenya is a good day. If Fremont were not my place, Kenya would be. It is my second home. I loved walking through the streets of Nyahururu with my friend Henry Waweru. I loved that Simon Mwaura could navigate the worst of Kenyan roads, and still couldn't find his way around Nairobi. I miss eating *noma choma* (roasted goat) with Wilfred, James, and their families at Ribs Village in Maralal.

God has blessed the work of T4 Global in East Africa in amazing ways. Selfishly, the most amazing way has been to drive home the lessons of Wendell

Berry in my own heart. Thinking in terms of tribe and place – and loving both for what they are – have been crucial lessons for me. The lessons of tribe and place showed up in a way and context I did not expect: my twenty-year high school reunion.

I was dreading my twenty-year reunion. For starters, I had gained about 100 pounds since I graduated, and lost my hair to boot. I could lie to you and tell you it's all good weight, but we won't go there. My lovely blonde mullet has been replaced by the middle-aged white guy head shave. I was also not ready to answer questions regarding what I did for a living. Most of the conversations started this way, "No really, Kyle. What do you do for a living? You're not really a pastor, are you?" I came braced for the worst.

God surprised me with the way He redeemed my dread. In the course of conversations with classmates, I learned something interesting. Most of the folks who grew up in either liberal, mainline Protestant churches, or in the Catholic church, had walked away from their faith. In high school, these people would self-identify with a church specifically, and loosely with the Christian faith. Now, they were Buddhist, or agnostic, or just "none of the above." While my tribe and my place boasted lots of churches (read "religion"), there was very little gospel. My classmates had found religion wanting, but they had not been introduced to Jesus.

If I had had that bit of information while in seminary, I would have thought, "Yet another reason I never want to go back to that dreadful place!" Now, however, Wendell Berry, Africa and, well, the Holy Spirit were doing something different in my heart. This news broke my heart. It caused something in me to cry out and long for a different story to tell for my place. As Amy and I talked on the way back to Kentucky, it became clear to me. I was flying all over the world, and was away from my family for extended periods of time so that other tribes could hear the gospel. *What about my tribe?* My tribe was chock full of religion, but had very little gospel. Liberal Protestant theology had so eviscerated the person and work of Jesus Christ that there was little left to follow.

Grace Church was planted out of that need; the desire to see the gospel planted in this place. At the end of the day, my call here is not really about planting a church. It's about seeing the gospel planted here in Fremont, and then watching what kind of community God raises up around the gospel. Christianity, historically, transforms a place. Prison reform, the abolitionist movement, hospitals, and universities all have Christian roots. I saw it in Africa, as well. The Good News transformed whole communities. Life was different and better because of the work of God in a particular place.

Gospel, People and Place
As a pastor, it's easy to love the gospel. It's harder to love the people you pastor, but it can be done. What is often forgotten is that we must also love the place in which God has called us to minister. We must work and pray for the well-being of our

place. The gospel will change not only individuals, but places as well.

I'm often asked, "Why does Fremont need another church?" My answer is: we don't. We need more gospel, more Jesus, but not more religious organizations. More technically, I can answer this way: the liberal Protestant churches in our town understand the *ethos* of this place well. What they have made a hash of, however, is the divine *Logos*. Grace Church was started because modern evangelicalism has a gnostic bent. The Bible-believing evangelical churches in town get the *Logos* right, but fail to love the *ethos* of our place. I know this because I was "that guy." For too long, I got the *Logos* right, but totally whiffed on the *ethos* of places like Elgin, Texas. I am a recovering gnostic.

By God's grace, don't be "that guy" too. Love the gospel. Love your people. Love the place. You belong and are part of a membership. The only question is whether you know it or not.

The myth of prophetic fits

While in seminary, my good friend and mentor, Paul House, presented a paper entitled "Crawford Howell Toy and the Weight of Hermeneutics." He told the story of Toy's dismissal from Southern Seminary in 1879 due to his embrace of higher critical methodologies. Toy's is a tragic story: not only did he lose his faculty position, but his engagement to famed Southern Baptist missionary Lottie Moon would end soon after as well. What stuck with me, however, is that Toy submitted his resignation to the board of trustees, expecting that they would not accept it. It was a paradigm that seemed to me to be right and proper. Toy did not really want to leave, but he did want to spare the institution the embarrassment of firing him. Much to his surprise and chagrin, they did indeed accept his resignation.

It is tempting, as pastors who are neck-deep in the trenches of difficult places of ministry, to have a C. H. Toy complex. When our methodology, our soteriology (any –ology, really) is questioned, we often respond with hurt and anger. To use a favorite southern expression of mine, "we pitch a fit." Now, we do indeed think such a fit is justified, even needed. After all, our integrity as a God-ordained minister of the gospel has been questioned! Pistols at dawn are not really an option, so we settle for pitching a good fit.

Twice I have handed in my resignation to deacon boards – and both times I felt justified in doing so. Why? Well, I was angry, and hurt, and confused. I was just done dealing with this particular brand of nonsense. In a self-righteous fit of arrogance, I had taken the "Toy Road." If these people cannot rightly appreciate the presence and ministry of the Lord's anointed, then I'll show them! I'll submit my resignation. Call their bluff, but show them I'm sick and tired of how my family and I are being treated.

Responding to stupidity with stupidity is rarely the course of godly wisdom. As I look back, I can see one of the issues much more clearly than I could before: there were expectations on both sides that were not being met. One of my reasons for leaving the denomination I was ministering in to enter the denomination in which I now minister is quite simple: I can deal with the expectations of this denomination.

Dealing well with expectations has multiple aspects to it. You must know what you do well;

you must be willing to honestly communicate your gifting up front to a prospective congregation. You also have to be willing to do a certain amount of necessary work, and be honest enough about your own gifting to know what you *can't* do. Finally, there needs to be some sort of regular framework through which you get feedback from the lay leadership at your church. Let's look at these in turn.

Play to Your Strengths

I urge guys starting out in ministry to do the following: find out what you're really good at. Find out what you love to do in ministry. God has wired and gifted you a particular way, and trying to minister outside of that gifting is foolishness. Once you've identified your gift and calling mix, do that. If you're not sure what it is, ask yourself the following question: what does my mind drift to as it relates to ministry? I found myself, as a youth minister, tucking a sermon in my Bible "just in case" the senior pastor was sick or had some sort of last-minute issue that prevented him from preaching. I would listen to our pastor preach and mentally work through how I would preach the same passage (I don't recommend this, by the way). As Kent Hughes used to say at the Wheaton Simeon Trust Workshop, "The pulpit calls the preacher as the sea calls a sailor. It will batter and bruise us, and we will love it for just that reason." Given the time and budget, I will always choose to read the latest book on preaching as opposed to the most recent book on any other topic or subject. Again, to quote Kent Hughes, "Preaching is both my greatest joy and my greatest burden." If that's not you, then you ought not pursue a ministry responsibility where preaching is your primary task. Preaching is what I love; it's what I think about when I'm not preaching. Any ministry where I'm not preaching on a regular basis is not sustainable long-term.

If you're married, your wife will be an invaluable source of feedback on this issue. Chances are, your wife knows you better than you know you. While in seminary, it's always a temptation to try to fit your calling to match the calling of a mentor or hero in ministry. I labored for quite some time thinking I would teach at the seminary level. After all, my closest seminary friends were either headed down the path to teaching, or currently teaching. My systematic theology professor told me, "You simply must go on and do further work." Providentially, however, I was able to attend the very first "Seminary Weekender" hosted by Mark Dever and the staff at Capitol Hill Baptist Church. Mark argued, quite persuasively, that the local church, not the academy, ought to be our first ministry option. My wife's encouragement, coupled with Mark's influence, quashed my misguided thoughts of Ph.D. work and a career in higher education. I'm grateful they did.

Own Your Weaknesses
Once you know your gift set and strengths, you have to winsomely but firmly communicate them. Be up front. Don't be timid or apologetic about it – let any prospective church know what you do

well. Be as blunt and passionate as you were when you were pursuing your wife! I pursued my wife with all the tact of a bulldozer. Hopefully, your denomination has some sort of instrument for you to communicate what you're good at and where your passions lie. In the PCA, it's called the MDF (Ministerial Data File). It gathers more than simply your strengths and weaknesses, but it does make sure all involved know what they're getting if they call you to minister. The PCA has no proprietary rights on the MDF, so it may be helpful to use it – even if you're already in a church.

Being up front and honest about yourself is hard. It's really hard if you don't have a job and you want one. It's even harder if you don't have a job and you NEED one. Some of us have the added burden of being people pleasers. We want people to like us. We make a hash of Paul's admonition to "be all things to all people." We know better, and yet some times we can't help ourselves. We agree too quickly to whatever we think the church or situation calls for, disregarding what we know to be true about ourselves. We must trust that God really is sovereign and that He really does love you and have a wonderful plan for your life. Trying to minister outside your gift mix is a sure-fire way to cause a train wreck. Causing that wreck will drive the people you desperately want to like you to hate your guts instead.

Get 'Er Done

Now of course, there are things that simply have to be done. It doesn't matter if you're good at them or not, they have to happen. Generally in churches, such yeoman's work falls squarely on the pastor's desk. I've learned, over time, to prioritize the things that I don't like and am not particularly good at. For example, I'm not an administrator. Bringing order out of chaos is not my gift. Because that's true, I give my Monday mornings to administrative tasks. That way, on the day I feel rotten anyway, I'm prioritizing my weakness.

This is also a great place for the body of Christ to function as it ought to function. One of the things I love about Grace Church is the way we "do work." The core group of our launch team knew what I was good at (preaching, teaching, and "that vision thing"). They also knew my weaknesses (administration, finances, technology "stuff"). I did not hide them, but stated them clearly. I also made sure they understood that for this plant to succeed, we would need to delegate, staff around, or otherwise deal with my weaknesses. Pastors are not omni-competent. The moment you truly realize this will be a blessed epiphany. The moment your church realizes this, you've got a puncher's chance at having a long and fruitful ministry in one place.

The end result has been beautiful to watch. Things that would take me all day to do and would still end up being done poorly are taken off my desk. This allows someone else to use his or her gift set/vocational skill set to serve the body of Christ. Everybody wins! Instead of asking someone to "do something for Jesus" that they're not gifted to do, give them work they can easily complete with a greater degree of skill and satisfaction than the pastor could ever muster.

Know What You Can't Do
Church planting is sexy. To paraphrase that great philosopher/male model Derek Zoolander, "Church planting – it's so hot right now." Let me say this as bluntly as I can: listening to Tim Keller or Mark Driscoll does not make you a church planter. Sporting a tat/multiple tattoos does not make you a church planter. Skinny jeans and flannel shirts do not make you a church planter. Sitting at a coffee shop and tweeting about how missional you are does not make you a church planter. Growing a sweet Duck Dynasty/Joe Thorn beard does not make you a church planter. Wanting really badly to be a church planter does not make you a church planter. Thinking that church planting is a really good idea does not make you a church planter. The Holy Spirit of God alone calls and gifts church planters.

Paul House, while teaching at Beeson Divinity School, has discovered an interesting thing about guys who want to plant a church: for many, it is a generational preference. These are guys who grew up in a culture of Internet start-ups. Spending an entire career with one company is no longer the "done" thing. You start something new; branch out on your own. Forget the established companies and organizations. Start small. Be flexible and agile. Build the better mousetrap. While this cultural and generational ethos removes some of the traditional fears associated with church planting, it is no substitute for the gifting and calling of the Holy Spirit.

Folks involved in church planting want to talk about how hard it is to be a church planter. Sure, OK. I will say this, however: it can be much harder to bring about the revitalization of a declining church than it is to plant a new one. I know this because I tried it and was no good at it. Why? Because that's not my calling or gifting. I lack the patience and people skills necessary for the work of revitalization. The moment I realized that was one of the most important in my ministry. It freed me to pursue what God had gifted me for: being the founding pastor of Grace Church.

As you learn how God has gifted you and seek opportunities to exercise those gifts, you have to become comfortable with the idea of turning down certain ministry responsibilities when they're outside your gift mix and calling. You have to be honest with yourself and trust the Lord's calling in your life to find what you've been called to do. Not everyone who wants to be a church planter is a church planter. Not everyone who wants to minister within higher education is called to the academy. Be realistic, and own what you can't do.

The funny thing about knowing what you can't do is that you are most likely already doing this – owning it – in other areas of life. For instance, I compete as a drug-free powerlifter. If you need heavy objects moved, call me. If you need someone to physically intimidate a young man giving unwanted attention to your teenage daughter, call me. If you need someone to handle the running leg of an Iron Man Triathlon, call my brother-in-law, Tim. Don't call me. Running is not my thing. I would no more consider running that race than Tim would consider putting on a squat suit and knee wraps to attempt a 600-lb squat. It's common sense, but I'm shocked how often we fail to apply common sense to ministry.

Only Half of the Equation
Knowing yourself and stating your expectations up front are only half of the story, however. The church or other ministry situation you are considering must be up front about what they expect of you. Experience tells me that congregations rarely do that well. If you ask them what they're looking for, they want a dynamic preacher and teacher, someone who is effective at personal evangelism, makes the visitation of the sick a priority, can handle all types of counseling, is a gifted administrator and visionary leader. They'd also like you to have all types of academic credentials, yet speaking the vocabulary of the "average guy." As for office hours, you ought to be in when folks stop by and they ought to see you out and about at various random community events. You ought to be out doing visitation several nights a week, and yet you're expected to be a good family man. In short, as a friend of mine once said, "I don't believe Billy Graham could satisfy what some of these folks want." Furthermore, if there are seven folks on the pastor search committee, there will be seven different opinions about which skill ought to be the priority. Needless to say, it takes a certain

amount of courage to start asking hard questions regarding what they expect. And to be prepared to hear and make sense of the answers.

Our consumer culture has done pastors little favors in this regard. The church growth movement has baptized "the consumer is always right" to the point that biblical standards for ministry have largely been jettisoned. What they really want, though it is rarely said, is for you to expand the ministry of their church. They want you to grow a big church and expand the programs offered so as to better attract other like-minded consumers. Granted, there ought to be some gospel to what is offered. If folks have tried everything else, they ought to try Jesus. Jesus will help their marriage, their kids, their finances, and their sex lives. You have the ultimate commodity. Market it well, or we'll find someone who will. Sadly, few congregations can discern their wants from their needs. They *want* to be a part of a large and growing church. They *need* a steady diet of Word and sacrament. They *want* to be told how the gospel helps them to be the best they can be. They *need* to be crushed by the law and revived by the gospel. Growth is usually a good thing, but we must help recover the conversation regarding church health as well as church growth.

Thankfully, the recovery of some biblical notions of church health has gotten traction within the evangelical world. There is a growing understanding that anonymity is not a New Testament value. Attending "relevant religious gatherings" with thousands of my "closest friends" does not lend itself to either gospel or human flourishing. The generations that have seen their families fall apart and have been marketed to from the moment they were born are looking for authentic community. Anonymity and community make strange bedfellows.

Start at the Very Beginning: Two Key Questions
I've learned two invaluable questions when dealing with search committees. The first one is, "Why am I of interest to you?" This may seem like a sad attempt to go fishing for a compliment, but how the question is answered will tell you a great deal about the congregation. If they say something like, "Well, you're a younger man with a younger family and we want more young families at our church ..." then you know you've got trouble on your hands. The demographic resemblance of the candidate to the group the church would like to reach is only one factor to take into consideration. There are a myriad of reasons that a particular church may not be attracting young families, such as location, lack of safe/well-staffed nursery services, or any number of other reasons. This can be a golden opportunity to have an "adult conversation" regarding reasonable expectations. As someone in vocational ministry, you may be aware of unspoken expectations that seem to be driving the conversation on their end. However, if the answer sounds in any way like, "Pied Piper" for a desired group, you may want to keep looking. The expectations may shift over time, but experience tells me this is rarely the case.

The second crucial question to ask is, "How will I know if I'm being successful?" If you've been up front with them about what they can expect from you, make sure there is some type of structure in place to give you feedback related to their expectations. If the answer is purely based upon numerical considerations, you may want to keep looking. If there is no method in place for the leadership structure, or the search committee, to give you an annual review, this is a good time to suggest that one is needed. I had a very candid conversation with a deacon at church #3 in which the deacon chair told me I "wasn't doing my job." Because I had been up front with them about what they could expect from me, I was able to say, "This is what I told you you'd be getting if you called me. Have I not done that?" He was able to admit that I had, but the deacons had changed their minds about what they thought this particular situation demanded from a pastor. It was not a pleasant conversation, but at least we both understood each other. Consequently, instead of "pitching a fit" and resigning, I was able to get some time to transition to a new place of ministry.

To Sum Up

Expectations are powerful things. When they're not met, we respond with great emotion. When there is nothing in place to discuss the expectations of the pastor and the congregation, these emotions can reach a boiling point over time. As I look back, I see how powerful and damaging unmet expectations can be. They brought my own level of frustration to the breaking point, and I was shocked when my frustrations were met with equal frustration. Both sides literally exploded at one another – and that is never a credit to the Body of Christ.

The steps I've suggested are not a foolproof scheme to make sure this does not happen to you. Search committees are in a rough place. They are asked to do a difficult job with no real guidance other than, "find our next pastor." My intention here is not to belittle their efforts and hard work. Rather, these steps are offered as a starting point for discussions that pastors and congregational leaders need to be having on a regular basis. Unleashing the fury of your unmet expectations upon lay leadership will feel cathartic for a microsecond. However, that catharsis will quickly be overwhelmed by shame and remorse. By God's grace, let us resolve to take steps to learn from the lesson of C. H. Toy. Pitching a fit will do more harm than good.

Jesus wants me to squat, bench, and deadlift

The Epiphany

Life-changing conversations ought to have some sort of theme music that accompany them.[1] Sadly, they never do. Such was the case when my friend Will Witherington was telling me about his golf game. This was a common occurrence, and while I enjoyed hearing about the latest game, I always wondered how he pulled it off. You see, Will is in (college) campus ministry. Since golf requires both time and money, I tend to view playing golf as a luxury, not a necessity – and certainly not something a campus minister would be well equipped to do regularly. Finally, I got up the nerve to ask him how in the world he played so much

---

1   Three words: '80s Hair Bands.

golf. Will's response was an epiphany for me. "I'm a competitive guy. Golf is my outlet. I'm a better husband and father – heck, I'm a better minister, because I have that outlet."

I was dumbstruck. The realization that I had been competing in ministry hit me immediately. If you don't already know this, competing in ministry is one of the dumbest things you could ever do. It's bad for your soul and for the souls of your folks. By trying to win, nobody wins.

As we think about the competitive nature of evangelical Christian culture at the beginning of the twenty-first century, we need a few basic guiding thoughts. First, we have to come to grips with how deeply this competitive ethos runs in American evangelical culture. We then have to recognize some of the well-intentioned but lame ways being offered to deal with this problem. Thirdly, we've got to find our golf game – our outlet. Finally, we need to put this competition syndrome with a larger context of balanced rhythms of life and ministry.

An Evangelical Malady

The really sad thing is that evangelical culture in America feeds the competitive tendency. We are numbers driven, and our model of what church should be often borrows more from Wall Street than from the New Testament. Woe to you who pastor small churches! The current climate within evangelicalism would lead one to believe that if a church is small, it's the pastor's fault. He's not prayerful enough, or gifted enough, or sold out enough, or dynamic enough, or _____ enough. If the pastor knew what he was doing, his church could be a mega church. Furthermore, there are plenty of mega church pastors who are willing for you to come to their conference so that you can learn their method for growing your church into the next great mega church. Get big, or go home!

If you live in a major metropolitan area, the pressure of the evangelical culture to grow your church into something of behemoth proportions is constant and unrelenting. In our consumer culture, folks will leave your church to go to another church that offers a wide variety of programming. If you try to take church discipline seriously, folks will flee to the anonymity of a mega church. If it's too far for you to drive to the "main campus," have no fear! We're opening a "satellite campus" (otherwise known as a franchise). Most American believers think as consumers first, Jesus-followers second. Sadly, the American evangelical movement has been more than willing to sanctify their consumerism in the name of Christianity.

As a competitive dude, I embraced the challenge. I'm a five-talent minister, after all. If I just work hard and smart enough, the church I pastor will be spoken of in hushed tones as the next rising congregation. I'll be hailed as some kind of genius and get invited to speak at the conferences with all my heroes. That sounds like a great idea, right?

A Bad Model and a Worse Life
One of the major problems with this kind of thinking and this model of church is that it

overlooks the fundamental nature of the church. Christ is the head of the church (Eph. 5:23). The competition/mega-church model presumes that I can build a congregation that looks like I want it to look. I, however, am not the boss of the church. I did not die to purchase the redemption of the church. My goal ought not to be numerical, but rather that Christ would bring His people to the congregation I pastor. The church will ultimately look like Christ wants it to look, not like I want it to look. I can't market or bottle that for others; I can only prayerfully depend on Jesus.

The stress of this kind of competing will be debilitating. It will lead to bad eating habits, ridiculous mood swings, and probably some type of sexual immorality (some guys go the "anonymous" route and turn to porn). This is model behavior if you're a MTV reality character, but deadly if you're a minister of the gospel.

Umm, What?

I love the academy. Some of my best friends make their living and serve the church within the academy. My sister-in-law and my two brothers-in-law work in higher education. God has used athletics and education to bring about almost every good thing in my life. I'm not an anti-academy guy.

It does make me scratch my head, however, when academicians feel the need to comment on the violent nature of some competitive sports (generally, American tackle football). Kent Hughes, in his excellent *Preaching the Word* commentary series, reminds us of Aristotle's *logos, pathos and ethos*. His application of this classical rhetorical theory as to preaching is brilliant, and it has far-reaching applications. In this instance, Aristotle cautions us against listening to guys who have never played a down/inning/quarter of competitive sports on any meaningful level. Why? They may be the smartest dudes in the room, and they may be quite sincere and passionate in their position, but their *ethos* is in the toilet. To quote a tweet from Anthony Bradley, "Academics and intellectuals are vulnerable to the self-deception that because they are competent in one area, they'll be competent in other areas."

The church, and the academic institutions that serve the evangelical church have bought into the competitive nature of twenty-first-century American culture. Hook. Line. Sinker. Go big, or go home. Demonizing violent forms of competition in an attempt to raise your own profile as an author/ professor/whatever simply demonstrates how inundated we are with this competitive ethos. The really sad thing is, the church as a whole struggles with attracting and discipling men. I'm not sure about the men at your church, but the men at Grace take the competitive (and violent) nature of life as a given. They embrace it, not because they love it (though some do), but because they have families to care for. Most of us don't kill our own food anymore, but the men in our church know something of the gumption required to keep a roof over people's heads, clothes on their backs, and food on the table. When non-athletes within the academy bash the violent nature of some competitive sports, they demonstrate two things many of us who love the academy already know. First, they demonstrate how out of touch academic sensibilities are with parish life. Second, they demonstrate how blind some folks can be to their own competitive tendencies – whether those are played out on the football field, or the academic field. So, trashing certain sports (usually a sport you've never played) to get your name out there is an acceptable form of competition? Oh, OK.

Rethinking Competition
There is, I think, a better option. Why not embrace the competitive nature of life in general? Granted, church is a rotten place in which to compete. There are bad and misguided models of competition out there, but what if we could use our competitive impulse to build healthy rhythms of life and ministry?

Local church ministry is not physically active work. We are, however, physical beings. Being physically active is of value to a minister of the gospel. So, what if we made our physical activity something that we could measure? What if it required planning on our part, and prioritizing our schedules to make sure that it happened on a regular basis? Planning, prioritizing, and measurable results sounds a lot like competition.

Saying that ministry is not physically active does not mean it's not physically taxing. The physiological strain of stress on ministers is a serious concern when it comes to long-term ministry. What I do mean is that most of us don't come home with sore muscles because we moved five loads of hay from the field to the barn. We weren't installing a boiler or bending electrical piping so we could run wire on a building remodel. We read, write, think, and talk for a living. Physicality is in somewhat short supply in our vocation.

I've always found lifting weights cathartic. It isn't just the physical part I enjoy, it's also the release of endorphins that accompanies weighted resistance training. Heavy squats are a venue in which Jesus and I have some of our most real and honest conversations. However, "working out" is not the same as training. I need the accountability of knowing I have a competition of some sort looming on the horizon. I need planning, prioritization, and measurable results.

I've found my "thing" competing as a drug-free powerlifter. To quote a tweet from bodybuilder Mark Dugdale (who is a believer), "Two things tend to put things in proper perspective – digging into the Bible and performing high rep. squats. Don't neglect either." You may not be a lifter, but you should find an avenue for competition outside of ministry. Within our presbytery, we have lots of runners. Personally, I find running annoying. I lack whatever thing it is that makes running enjoyable to someone. Put 500 pounds on my back and tell me to squat past parallel and stand up? That's a different story altogether. My friend Will Witherington plays golf. Brothers in our presbytery run half and full marathons. I lift. I'm not arguing that lifting is better than the others (it is for me). But I am arguing that you need to find your thing. Run, play golf, play tennis, lift, whatever. Raise your level of general physical preparedness. Plan, prioritize, and keep score. You'll feel better physically, emotionally, and spiritually.

Next Steps

My conversation with Will got me thinking on a particular track, but it was the GCA Conference in Orlando that helped to round out my thinking on this crucial lesson in ministry. GCA stands for Global Church Advancement, and it's a terrific church-planting workshop put on by Steve Childers and some other folks who have a loose affiliation with Reformed Theological Seminary – Orlando. In his final talk, Steve talks about the importance of the "Seven 'S's" in ministry. These are sleep, sun, solitude, Sabbath rhythm, sexual intimacy, sweat, and swallow. In other words, if you're not getting enough sleep, getting outside and catching some Vitamin D via the sunlight, getting alone for a particular season of time, taking time to rest and worship, being intimate and romantic with your spouse, getting some exercise, and not stuffing your face on a regular basis, you will not do very well in ministry over the long haul. Amy and I quickly added an eighth "s" – solvent. Life in ministry can be challenging financially, and the stress of financial worries can suck the life and joy out of your marriage and ministry.

One of the great gnostic lies the church has swallowed unquestioningly is the idea that we are not whole people. When you combine our gnostic tendencies with the consumer mantra, "you *can* have it all," you have a recipe for disaster. We neglect particular areas of our lives in pursuit of a generic, culture-defined version of having everything. Trying to have it all is a great way to end up with a glorious nervous breakdown, a stroke, or a heart attack.

Ministers must be intentional and almost obsessive about prioritizing their lives in order to be balanced. We must set our priorities and then set our schedules according to those priorities. When you feel like your head is about to explode, a quick check of the "Eight 'S's" will let you know where your life has gotten out of balance. If we let the tyranny of the urgent set our schedules, we will be running around playing fireman in an endless loop of frustration. Sit down with your wife first and get her input. One of reasons I married my wife is that we are opposites, and therefore, we make a great team. She knows me better than I know myself, and most importantly, she loves me unconditionally. Her input on how to balance my life via the "Eight 'S's" is crucial.

I've discovered another crucial benefit in this process. In the past, I failed to understand how much of Amy's stress was related to my well-being and the well-being of our family. I've also found that this is true of good wives in general. They want their husbands and their families healthy and doing well. When it's not so, their stress levels go up correspondingly. When Amy gave voice to her concerns about our finances, or my well-being, it sounded to me like nagging. Dudes hate nagging. Now, it wasn't nagging, but we had nothing in our married life that provided a chance for us to examine the "Eight 'S's" together. We now have an annual financial planning meeting with one of our ruling elders. We sit down and look at our calendar at the beginning of the year and lay out the commitments we know we have. Decisions on what to add or remove are made as we examine our family calendar with the "Eight 'S's" in mind. Our marriage and daily life in the McClellan house is better for it.

Once your wife is on board, sit down with your leadership structure within your church. If you've been competing via church, own it! Confess it to them, and model repentance for them. Lay out the "Eight 'S's" to them, and ask for feedback and guidance on how to embrace a balanced model of competition for life and ministry. Many of them have careers that will use them unmercifully. Balance is not just something a pastor needs; it's something we all need. Having this discussion with your leadership team can become a real and authentic means to introduce biblical priorities into everyday life. You can help your leaders embrace competition in a God-honoring, balanced way! Remember, competition does not mean proving I'm better than you. Rather, competition is the application of planning and prioritization to get a measured result. My guess would be that your leadership team would be positively impacted if each man sat down with his wife for a time of planning, prioritizing, and deciding upon a measured result in the "Eight 'S's". How different would the evangelical church look if we as leaders competed in this way?

Too Bad Pastors' Meeting Can't Be This Way

I love meet day! There is nothing like devoting eight to twelve weeks of training to get ready for a particular meet and then going out and letting the big dog eat! All the hard work and preparation means that when you step onto the platform to hit your opening squat, you have laser-type focus. Nothing matters at that moment except smoking that first squat.

You would think such a testosterone-charged, pre-workout-fueled[2] atmosphere would be filled with negative examples of competition. There must be guys talking smack, or trying to get into other dudes' heads. Now sadly, 'roid rage is nobody's friend, but among drug-free powerlifters an interesting thing happens on meet days: your competition cheers for you. No one is yelling, "Miss it!" In fact, just the opposite is true. Guys love it when a dude just goes off at a meet. Why? You understand just how hard the other guy worked to get there. You know the sacrifice it takes to legally bench press 400 pounds. You respect the

---

2 There is an entire line of supplements designed to be taken before a workout. In theory, they boost your mental focus and prepare your central nervous system for the beating it's about to take. Think powdered Red Bull.

hard work and the effort it takes for a lifter to set a personal record. There is a spirit of camaraderie that is infectious.

What if pastors' meetings within your denomination were that way? What if leadership meetings within your church were that way? What if the 300-pound deacon who broke a sweat tying his shoes lost fifty pounds in six months and his annual physical was no longer a "come-to-Jesus" meeting? What if the elder who had been a complete tool to his co-workers found a better, healthier outlet for his competitive juices? What if the wives of your lay leaders sent you emails thanking you for introducing them to a way in which they could help guide their families in a way that was not perceived as nagging? What if guys were sharing redemptive stories about how their lives were different because they have embraced a balanced, healthy approach to competition?

For too long, I embraced the same model of competition that evangelical Christian culture is "ate up with." Once I realized I needed a physical release that required planning, prioritizing, and measured results, it was a life- and ministry-changing event. Once Amy and I realized that the "Eight 'S's" gave us the chance as husband and wife to go hard after balanced and healthy rhythms of life and ministry, our marriage has not been the same.

LESSON FIVE

Find your preaching voice
— not someone else's

Imitation is indeed the sincerest form of flattery. Early in ministry, if you had been listening closely, you would have been able to identify whom I'd been listening to that week. Alistair Begg, Mark Dever, John Piper, and Kent Hughes formed my preaching "Super Friends." My preaching reflected not my own style, but theirs.

Some of this is to be expected. After all, there are plenty of fields of endeavor in which you pattern what you would like to be after the work of someone else. Plenty of aspiring guitar players copy the virtuosity of one Eddie Van Halen, or the classical styling of Christopher Parkening. Our son has just started playing the drums. His YouTube play list includes drummers he'd like to sound like: Manu Katché, Dave Weckl, Vinnie Colaiuta, Max Weinberg, the late Jeff Porcaro, and Aaron

Mellengårdh from Dirty Loops. He'll never sound *exactly* like any one of these guys, but he's imitating the playing style of each one. Young athletes do this all the time: in my generation, every good basketball player wore Michael Jordan's 23 and sported a pair of Air Jordans. Young soccer players want to "bend it like Beckham." As we are learning and hoping to master any complex skill, we look for good models after which we may pattern our own work.

My own growth as a preacher has been worked out of an experiential understanding of what it means to preach rightly. In other words, as my definition of preaching has solidified, I've been able to find my own voice. As I listen to young preachers, I recognize a similar need in their preaching. They're not sure who they are (more on that later), they're not sure what they're supposed to be doing, and so they fall into imitation. As D. A. Carson reminded folks at the 2011 Gospel Coalition meeting while introducing Tim Keller, "Don't try to out-Keller Tim Keller. You'll just sound foolish."

What Else You Got?

For many years now one of my preaching heroes, Alistair Begg, would begin sermons about the nature and task of preaching by modifying a quote from W. E. Sangster: "Preaching is in the shadows. The world does not believe in it." This was Sangster's sentiment in 1954. Begg has updated the quote this way, "Preaching is in the shadows, but this time much of the church does not believe in it."[1]

---

1   Alistair Begg, *Preaching for God's Glory* (Crossway: Wheaton, IL; 2010), p. 13.

While there are reasons for hope within evangelical circles, I fear Alistair is largely correct.

Our confusion about preaching is part of a larger picture of uncertainty. Much of the evangelical church is confused regarding what corporate times of worship are really supposed to do. Isaac Wardell's helpful study, *Liturgy, Music and Space*,[2] introduces us to three helpful metaphors for what goes on when God's people gather together: a lecture hall, a concert hall, or a banquet hall. Eventually, the preacher conforms what he does when he stands to speak to fit the expectation of the hall in which he finds himself. Lecture Hall guys view preaching as a theological discourse, and Concert Hall guys want to keep the mojo of the concert going. It's only the Banquet Hall motif that gives preaching its rightful place within the larger context of God's people gathering together week by week. Let's look at the first two examples as we think about what preaching is *not*.

The Lecture Hall
Within the tradition I now minister in, there are young guys who view preaching as a lecture in systematic theology. The goal of the sermon is to either teach sound theology outright, or to replace bad theology with a more "kosher" version. These guys are easy to spot – generally because they're trying to cram as much information, and as many words as possible, into their allotted time.

---

2   www.bifrostarts.com

This is not to refute or minimize the need for good theology. Indeed, one of the reasons preaching is in the shadows within some churches is precisely because of bad theology. One of the classic models from the Proclamation Trust/Simeon Trust will help us stay balanced: we must have a large "T" (text) and a small "f" (theological framework). The point of the sermon is not to shed more light on a particular doctrinal point. The point of the sermon ought to be to make the meaning of the text known to your listeners. If there is particular doctrine that flows out of a text, then make it known. Our job, however, is to proclaim the text first and foremost.

Sometimes, the framework being imposed upon the text – and therefore, the listener – does not fall into the category of systematic theology. Bryan Chapell's "fallen condition focus" (FCF)[3] is a wonderful reminder that we must ultimately get to the gospel in our preaching. However, I've sat through too many ordination sermons in which the FCF rides roughshod over an Old Testament text. The preacher goes into the text looking for their FCF – not seeking to understand what the text itself says. Ultimately, the FCF is a good tool for helping us apply the text, but it's crummy as a hermeneutical tool. We must get to Christ in our application, but we must first understand the text.

The Concert Hall

Concert Hall preachers remind us, and rightfully so, that preaching is a unique experience each and every time the audience comes together. Christianity

---

3   Bryan Chapell, *Christ Centered Preaching* (Baker: Grand Rapids, MI, 1994).

must be lived out, and the truth ought to move us emotionally. If the Lecture Hall guys tend to view us as having huge intellects and small hearts/emotions, then the Concert Hall guys view the audience as having big emotions and small intellects. The experience is the thing. Your "worship team" has set the stage and prepared your audience. Now, you must move them to the next step through your words and delivery. Generally speaking, when Concert Hall speakers stand to give their pitch, there is an element of sanctified marketing to religious consumers lurking in the background.

Such preaching, while helpfully reminding us of the unique experience of each Sunday, starts in the wrong place. The wants and emotional state of the audience is not where a preacher starts. We start with God's Word, and stand and prayerfully declare that Word to God's people. Preachers are not "life coaches" or "motivational speakers" or any other such nonsense. You did not call yourself into ministry – so the idea that you define the ministry to which you have been called is idolatrous rot. The Puritan Thomas Carlyle spoke words that ought to stop such foolishness: "Who, being called to be a preacher, would stoop to be King?"[4]

Ironically, most Concert Hall guys will tell you they believe in the inerrancy of God's Word. Their problem, however, is that they don't believe in the sufficiency of that Word. The reliance is not upon

---

4   Christopher Ash, *The Priority of Preaching* (Proclamation Trust Media/ Christian Focus: 2010), p. 25.

the Spirit of God using the Word of God to call into existence God's particular people. Rather, the reliance is on relevant communication. If I can move you emotionally, then I've done my job. The fact that Genesis 3:6 teaches us that what we see, feel, and approve must be submitted to the higher authority of the Word of God is apparently lost on the Concert Hall crowd.

The Lecture Hall and Concert Hall models share another unintended commonality: both let the congregants come as spectators. We've all been to concerts (especially classical concerts) where you come and sit quietly. Granted, Springsteen will have you singing along; but unless you're Courtney Cox and we're filming the "Dancing in the Dark" video, don't think you're going on stage with Bruce and the E Street Band. We've all also been to class and sat quietly in the back, dutifully taking notes while the professor droned on and on about something or the other. In both instances, we're spectators. Our participation is welcome, but optional.

The Banquet Hall

Wardell's third image is that of the Banquet Hall. The Banquet Hall engages the whole person. When God's people gather each week, they are coming to "taste and see that the Lord is good" (Ps. 34:8 NIV). Each course of a banquet adds to the experience of the whole. In Banquet Hall thinking, the gospel is sung, read, prayed, and recited long before the preacher stands to proclaim the Word of God. God's people are invited to sing, pray, and respond to the reading of God's Word before the preaching event. The preaching of the Word is not the only gospel event in the course of a given gathering. The whole service is a gospel service, and that service – like a banquet – engages the whole person. Many Banquet Hall congregations celebrate the Lord's Supper on a weekly basis. This is yet another way God's people are actively engaged as they gather. They are much more than spectators.

One may go to a concert and sit quietly. One may attend a lecture and be disengaged. It is much harder to attend a banquet and not participate. The smells, sights, and tastes of the entire event engage the whole person. The soup may not have been to your liking, but there are several other courses yet to come. The main course is still the preaching of God's Word (contra Concert Hall), but we value the other courses for the contribution they make to the whole (contra Lecture Hall).

Knowing Which Hall You're In
If your preaching will eventually reflect the context in which you minister week after week, you will want to give careful consideration to the hall in which you find yourself. A dear friend of mine is an excellent preacher with Lecture Hall tendencies. He recently took a position with a church that has a Concert Hall approach to ministry. His preaching will come as a shock to some within that congregation, as well as to the church musicians. He was upfront about the kind of ministry they could expect from him, but there will be a period of

adjustment for both pastor and congregation. One does not move from hall to hall easily.

A Working Definition
Knowing the hall you're in is only half the battle. You must have a working definition of preaching regardless of your hall affiliation. Preaching is what I spend most of my time doing, preparing to do, and thinking about when I'm not doing. As I've wrestled with what preaching is, I've come to this working definition: *Preaching is the division, explanation, and application of the Bible so that God's self-revelation is intelligible in a particular context.* Let's unpack that definition a bit more.

The first half of the definition is a bit vanilla, I know. There's nothing original or earth-shattering about such an approach to preaching. However, there is always the danger that we make preaching about something other than the text. The task of the preacher is to divide, explain, and apply **the Bible**. Not a particular confession of faith. Not a systematic theology. Not a helpful book or philosophical approach to life. The text must reign supreme when a preacher steps forward to speak. This implies a confidence in the Word of God, as well as a willingness by the congregation to sit under that Word.

It's the second half of the definition that needs to be unpacked. What do we mean by *intelligible in a particular context*? I learned all I think I know about intelligibility working for T4 Global.[5] T4 is an orality-based missions organization that does

---

5   For more, please go to www.t4global.org.

its best work among unreached or least-reached people groups. Orality is a fascinating piece of the modern missiological puzzle. Oral culture peoples are those whose preferred way of gaining, processing, and passing along information is through non-literate means. Songs, stories, dance, and proverbs play a huge role in oral cultures. For the Christian missionary, this is good news! After all, three-fourths of the Bible is narrative. The Bible contains wisdom sayings as well as songs. At the risk of sounding contradictory, the Bible is an extremely oral piece of literature.

T4 Global treats oral culture folks like people, not like idiots who someday need to be taught to read. The stories and songs that are utilized are always in the tribal tongue, not the *lingua franca*. The life-changing story of the gospel comes home in their language, in a way they understand and prefer to communicate. When the orality mojo works, it's a powerful and beautiful thing! Orality is a powerful tool, and the guys at T4 wield that tool with great skill.

For too long, Western missionaries have approached oral culture peoples with a literate gospel. While reading is a good thing, and there are undeniable economic advantages to being literate, literacy ought not to be a prerequisite for hearing and understanding the gospel. Even in our oral presentations of the gospel, we present an essentially literate message – which is then unintelligible in an oral culture context.

Perhaps an example would help, such as that of our church partners with an indigenous network of churches in Kenya. God's Grace for All Nations (GGFAN) is committed to taking the gospel to the twenty-two unreached tribes in Kenya. As with most indigenous, developing-world groups, GGFAN used borrowed Western methodologies in their attempts to share the gospel. They used door-to-door evangelism: specifically, a brief, easily memorized presentation of the gospel. Beginning with the question, "Do you know Jesus?" the presenters would give their gospel talk.

One man was quite helpful in his response to their presentation: He had not, in fact, ever met this Jesus. But, since these gentlemen were obviously looking for him, they might enquire in the next village over. It was a bigger village, and got news quicker than their village did. He hoped they would find this Jesus, since he did indeed sound like an interesting fellow. One other gentleman was certain they were stumping for a political candidate, and pledged to vote for Jesus as the Member of Parliament candidate from their district! Whatever these sincere and committed pastors thought they were sharing with folks, it clearly was not the gospel that was being communicated. While their gospel presentation would have been intelligible in a Western context, it made no sense in an African context. I fear much of our preaching has the same impact.

One question I've found to be invaluable in thinking about intelligibility for our context is this: *What am I presuming people know when I speak?* Most preachers use a particular kind of Christian lingo when we preach. When we use those terms, we presume our folks come with a mutual definition and understanding of the term. Experience has taught me we ought not do so. Intelligibility means we leave the lingo aside and do the hard work of a wordsmith for our congregation. It means we leave the technical speak we learned to love in seminary aside, and speak plainly in non-technical terms. Since we know that the Spirit of God always accompanies the preaching of the Word of God, we can press on knowing that God will do His work – even if we make a hash of things.

The Most Helpful Meeting of My Week
One of the most fruitful seasons of preaching in my ministry came when I was getting regular feedback. My good friend Richard Bailey and I would meet every Thursday morning at Heine Brothers Coffee in Louisville. We would debrief the sermon from the week before, and then talk about the sermon for the upcoming Sunday. Thursday was a great day: it was far enough removed from the previous week's sermon that I could be objective about how the sermon had really gone. It was also close enough to the coming Sunday that the majority of my preparation had already been done. I could receive feedback without feeling threatened, and I had the bulk of my sermon prep done, so I was able to discuss where the next sermon was going.

You ought to find your Richard Bailey. This will need to be someone who shares your working definition of preaching, and whom you trust. Preaching is an intensely personal endeavor. We easily hear, "I didn't like that sermon" as "I don't like you." Richard is a dear friend, and he wanted for both the gospel to be heard, and for me to grow and do well as a preacher. He could be clear and direct in his feedback, but he also spoke as someone who loved me and whose ultimate aim was to encourage. It's hard and at times painful to listen to honest feedback, but you'll be a better preacher for doing so.

This is also a place where our wives can be of great help. Amy is easily my most balanced critic. She knows my insecurities and how those insecurities will surface in my preaching. She knows when I'm nervous, even when no one else does. She knows the inner workings of our house and how that will affect the preaching of the Word. In short, she knows me better than anyone else. She knows if she's hearing *me*, or if she's hearing a cheap Kent Hughes knock-off.

Not a Microwave Dish

Developing your own voice takes time. You must preach often and regularly to find it. You must have a clear definition of preaching as you do so, and you must know the kind of hall in which you're preaching. Feedback from a trusted friend who shares your working definition of preaching is invaluable, and your wife will also be a valuable sounding board as you go about this process.

However, like any complex skill, finding your own voice will not happen overnight. Both of my grandfathers were skilled tradesmen. One was a plumber/steamfitter and the other a heavy diesel mechanic. They worked hard at their prospective crafts. What they did not do was master their trade overnight. They devoted their lives to learning their craft. I keep my Grandpa Carlson's work jacket in my office. It reminds me of the family legacy I possess: it's a good thing to devote one's life to mastering a particular craft.

Young preacher, you're not the second coming of Spurgeon or Lloyd-Jones or Keller. You have a lifetime of preaching ahead of you. Kent Hughes used to open the Simeon Trust workshops by reminding us that as a preacher, he was better at fifty than he was at age forty. He was better at forty than he was at thirty. Folks with an athletic background will tell you this is counterintuitive. David Beckham is not as good now as he was ten years ago. Michael Jordan with the Washington Wizards was painful to watch. Golfing great Ben Hogan developed the "yips" and could not putt by the end of his illustrious career. Preaching, however, is different. Work hard at this good craft. You have a lifetime to find your own voice. By God's grace, you'll get better as you get older.

LESSON SIX

Live on the knife-edge of authenticity and godliness

Be yourself; everyone else is already taken.

– Oscar Wilde.

"The ministry tends to attract insecure narcissists." I wish I could put my name behind that quote, but my friend and fellow church planter Christopher Robins gets credit for that one. It's a great quote because it's accurate and honest. Most of us want to be accurate and honest as pastors, but we're not sure if our folks would receive it well. I think this is one reason why so many guys plant churches. If you start a new church, there is no predecessor to set the bar regarding how the pastor is supposed to conduct himself. At a certain level, folks who are drawn to the new church are drawn to the founding pastor's vision, the founding pastor's personality, and the founding pastor's whole way of doing things. It's both liberating and dangerous. While I need to be me, being me is not always helpful, edifying, or Christ-exalting.

Good models are important. You'll spend a great deal of your life either trying to figure out how your models have contributed to your proclivity to be a train wreck, or how your models have served your pursuit of general awesomeness. I knew this early on – but there was a problem. I couldn't find a model in ministry that I felt connected to on a personal level. Sure, there were guys whose preaching I liked. There were guys whose gear was tight in the pulpit. There were guys who had lives I thought I would like to have, but I could not find one that fit me in totality. Granted, this may imply an overinflated sense of me, but if you've read this far, this is not a shocking revelation.

When I was in high school, my small town version of American culture wanted you to fit neatly in categories. I played football, but had friends who weren't football players. I played in the band, but had friends who were not "bandies." I was in some AP (advanced placement) classes with the smart kids, but took remedial math fit for kids young enough to write with crayons. Am I a jock/bandie/smart kid/not so smart kid/Jesus follower? Which category do I fit? I didn't fit any one category. I wanted to, but I didn't. It was not a good or helpful phase in my life.

In some ways, I still really struggle with this. Not many pastors are reading A. S. Prilepin[1] *and* Carl F. H. Henry. Not many pastors can help sort cattle

---

[1] Prilepin is a Russian strength coach/evil genius. The volume in his programming is brutal, but the results more than speak for themselves on meet day.

and then head to the comic book store to see if the "New 52" Green Arrow has arrived. I've been told I preach "like a Baptist," but was also told I don't "sound like a Baptist." Huh? Now, I'm just more comfortable with not fitting any category cleanly. Not many guys are pursuing the following: their wife, seeing the gospel planted in a particular place, a D.Min., and a 700-pound squat. If I try to remove any of those things, I feel like I'm going to lose my mind. If I try to fit in neatly in a category, it's no good. If, on the other hand, I try to be a rebel and self-consciously "transcend and defy categories," I'm being a pretentious bore. Again, don't be "that guy."

Public Expectations

Expectations are powerful things. When I went on a church staff as "the youth guy," the expectation was that you were a goofball. Eventually you would figure out what you wanted to do when you grew up. For most guys, youth/college ministry has a shelf life. When I looked at the senior pastors I served under, there were certain elements of their lives and ministry that I liked, but nothing in the totality of how they went about their lives and ministry. They were good and godly men, but totally unlike me. I was trying to figure out how I could be authentic and relatable, but not such a total jerk most of the time. This was hard and frustrating work.

Pretty soon the unthinkable happened: the good folks at the Orville Baptist Church called me to be their senior pastor. I knew I could not rock the "youth pastor" persona, but what *did* they expect?

If I could even decipher their expectations, could I meet them? Thankfully, but not helpfully in the long term, Orville just wanted me to be me. Me, however, is not always a helpful thing.

I think lots of guys starting out in ministry struggle with this. It's why so many guys try to sound and dress like Mark Driscoll. It's why so many young guys at Southern Seminary dress and conduct themselves like Al Mohler. It's why so many young guys at the PCA's General Assembly sport a bow tie. It's what their hero/mentor does, so it's what they do. They conduct themselves like those they admire. Hopefully, the model is good and it fits you. When it doesn't (and it never fully does), you end up confused and embarrassed. You are play-acting. You know it. Your wife knows it. Deep down, the folks who are paying attention know it as well. Ministry is hard. Trying to "do ministry" as someone else is impossible.

My Way or Jesus' Way?
There is a solution to all this. It's not trendy or sexy. It does not involve particular habits of haberdashery or the exclusive use of a Moleskine notebook. Find who Jesus has made you to be. Crazy, right? It took me a long time to figure this one out. For so long, I was trying to either be someone else or to be the guy I thought my parishioners wanted me to be. I was miserable and incompetent at both.

As I look back upon my life as a Jesus-follower, not just as a pastor, there is a disappointing theme that emerges. I'm not a very good disciple. The ups and downs in my life generally, and in ministry in particular, tend to coincide with my walk with Jesus. When I neglect the basic means of grace in my relationship with Jesus, I'm a jerk. My tendency is to try to be someone else. I'm a crummy husband and an unengaged father. When, however, I'm utilizing the means of grace that I've been given as a Jesus-follower, things are better. I'm still kind of a jerk, but my jerkiness is mitigated by the presence of the resurrected Christ in me. When I try to be the Great Plains version of Tim Keller, I'm a phony and a loser. Furthermore, the folks at Grace don't need Keller to pastor them. They need the guy Jesus has actually called to be their pastor. It's a bum deal for them, but Jesus called me.

What about you? If I asked you about your devotional habits, could you give an honest answer that actually reflected what you habitually do, or would I hear pious nonsense? If I asked you about your habits of Sabbath and solitude, what would you say? I've learned the hard way that I cannot grumble at the presence and damage done by sin in my life but turn my back on reading God's Word and prayer. Stop reading angry blogs and start reading John Owen. Pursue Jesus like your life depends upon it, because it does.

Really Me

As I pursue my relationship with Jesus with some sort of consistency and discipline, I figure out who I am. I am reminded that the folks at Grace need me to pastor them. Not the fake me, or the me who wants to be someone else. The real me. This means I need to be really good at repenting in front of my folks. Why? The real me is a work in progress. As much as I might think people want to be around my awesomeness, not every part of my personality is helpful or edifying.[2] The Holy Spirit is engaged in the same work of sanctification in my life as He is in everyone else's. This is the knife-edge: how to pastor in a way that is really and authentically me while still being a guy who needs the gospel proclaimed to him as much as anyone else.

We've tried to capture this idea in the core values of Grace Church. We want to be a place where, "It's OK not to be OK, but not OK to stay that way." I'm not the only one who needs to live on the knife-edge. We all do. We all need to be genuine and authentic. We all need to pursue Jesus because our genuine and authentic self is a redeemed sinner. We need to be good at repenting in front of one another. We need to be equally good at forgiving and bestowing grace on folks whose authenticity offends us. It becomes the ethos of your community. It's not clean or easy, but it is refreshing and, we think, life-giving. Jesus died to clean up your mess. Stop trying to clean it up yourself.

Learning the Hard Way
I wish I could spare you one of the most awful experiences in all of ministry: criticism. You will

---

2   For instance, sarcasm is my love language. To paraphrase Sammy Kershaw's "Queen of my Doublewide Trailer", *I'm the Charlie Daniels of sarcasm.* Sarcasm can be effective when used wisely and sparingly. I rarely do either.

be criticized. Sadly, it comes with the territory. Hopefully, the criticism is aimed at you and not your family. But what makes criticism especially difficult is if the thing that is being criticized isn't even you in the first place. I have had the rotten experience of being criticized, all the while knowing that what they were criticizing wasn't really me! It's one thing to call me on something if it really is me, but it is an absolutely soul-wrenching experience to be called on something that isn't really you. This is when it becomes clear that all you are doing is play-acting. You're trying to be someone else, or you're trying to be the guy you think your church wants you to be. Take it from me: please, please, please: don't do it! Be you. Christ died for you. He called you to your place of ministry. Your people need you to minister to them, not a cheap knock-off of somebody else. Jesus began a good work in you. He is faithful and He will complete the good work. Use the means of grace He has given you. Live on the knife-edge.

LESSON SEVEN

Try not to be a train wreck as a husband and father

I never meant to be so bad to you/One thing I said that I would never do. – Asia

This is, for many reasons, the most difficult chapter to write. My sin and stupidity affect ministry, as well as me personally, in a multitude of ways. However, the fact that my sin, failure, and shortcomings also impact my family is a most painful reality. The people I love the most are the ones most impacted by my lack of Christ-likeness. Over time, I've come to realize that I'm not alone in this: pastors can often be crummy husbands and fathers. While this does not excuse our shortcomings, there is some comfort in knowing we're not alone in our awfulness. But, if this seems to be pandemic to ministry, it does drive me to want to ask: Why? Why do pastors often make bad husbands and fathers? Why, when one of the requirements to serve God's people is that we "manage his own household well" (1 Tim. 3:4)? It would seem that we'd be really good at this, seeing as how it is a prerequisite for pastoral ministry and all. Sadly, we're not. It pains me that this impacts the Kingdom. It kills me to see the effect of this in the faces of my wife and kids.

This is also the chapter that is the most fluid and open-ended for me. The other chapters reflect some finality with respect to my thinking and experience. I know and have worked through the issue. My convictions are firm. I'd like to think that my perception of the issue is clear. This does not mean that I think I have arrived – but I do have some clarity on the issues. I can see a way forward. I make no such claims as I think about my family. I love them, want to serve and do right by them, but our life together is very much a work in progress.

What I Know and What I Think I Know
Thinking about the mystery of marriage falls into two general categories: there are things I know and there are things I think I know. What I am certain of is what God has revealed about marriage in His Word. What I think I know is the experiential working out of biblical truth in our marriage particularly. Where most of us get into trouble is when we confuse the two. This problem is further compounded because pastors are prone to such categorical confusion on a regular basis. We often confuse our pontificating about the Bible with the Bible. Disaster inevitably follows.

Let's start with the positive: marriage is a divinely instituted union. This is not the invention of a particular culture. Humanity did not come up with the idea of marriage on its own. Revisiting the Genesis account is a helpful exercise; for it's there that we learn that marriage is God's answer to a pressing human need. In a narrative filled with *tov* (good) we suddenly run into a *lo tov* (not good). Eve is a walking, talking, breathing reminder of God's love and care for Adam. She was not Plan B or a consolation prize. Eve is the pinnacle of God's good creation and a gift to Adam. Adam receives her as such and cherishes her appropriately.

When my life with Amy goes astray, it's often because I've forgotten this basic and fundamental fact. My wife is a walking, talking, breathing reminder of God's love, grace, and mercy to me. She is a gift. Treating the gift poorly is, generally speaking, an indication of our regard for the giver. My most cherished gifts are not the most spectacular, or the most expensive. Rather, they are from *people* I love and cherish. The gift is an expression of love and a reflection of our life together. Gut check #1 is usually my relationship with God. When I treat Amy poorly, or take her for granted, it's usually because I'm neglecting my relationship with God.

What I think I know numbers only two things. If God grants us another two decades of marriage, I'm sure that number will go down! When we were first married, I kind of thought I could figure this marriage thing out quickly. I had a game plan, a point-by-point plan of attack. It was sheer idiotic hubris. Thankfully, the list has been shrinking. So, what do I think I know? I think I know that I need to be a student of Amy's family, and that I need to reprioritize my vocational calling.

Be a Student of Your Wife's Family
You could not possibly pick two families that are more different than our respective families. I think it's probably easier to list what they have in common: both sets of parents are Jesus-followers, and we both come from intact households (our folks are still married). That's it! Amy is the middle of three girls. I am the oldest of four kids: two boys and two girls. We're the only members of my extended family to move back to Nebraska. We're the only members of Amy's extended family to leave Kentucky. I could go on, but I think you get the picture.

Early in our married life, I viewed the differences as being bad – but in a selfishly skewed way. It was Amy's family that was weird, not mine! I would see mannerisms or thought processes that were familial in my wife and think, "Wow! That's so your mom/dad!" I quickly learned that giving voice to such thoughts is never helpful. Your wife loves you; so don't make her choose between you and her parents/siblings. The reality of leaving and cleaving takes time, and you're not helping the process by pointing out comparisons with her family of origin – at all.

The familial differences showed up in more harmful ways, however. We grew up with very different models for how a husband and wife deal with conflict. We had very different ideas about parenting, education, sports, and a whole list of other topics that married couples need to discuss and navigate. On top of that, marriage is a marvelous institution for exposing our own selfishness and stupidity! Conflict would arise, and we would respond in keeping with the model we had seen growing up. The problem was, those models were really, really different. This added to the frustration and conflict. The loop was now set, and we could not seem to get out of it.

Being a student of your spouse's family of origin does not mean you're going to nitpick or that you're trying to demonstrate whose family is superior or right. It means that I want to understand why Amy responds to certain situations the way she does. We all have a "default" setting. For most of us, our default setting was formed in our family of origin. When the stress and conflict of marriage sets in, that's where we instinctively go. I need to know Amy's default settings and figure out why they're set the way they are. To do so, I need to become a student of her family. I need to pay attention to actions and attitudes that show up in the course of everyday life. Once I started doing so, and stopped lamenting the differences, it helped me understand my wife. It was a good step in being able to "live with [my wife] in an understanding fashion" (to paraphrase 1 Pet. 3:7).

A note of caution: understanding and articulating are two different disciplines. You must guard against pride and hubris when undertaking this type of study. One can easily get to, "It's so sad. I know why you do this, but you have no idea.

I must be smarter/more self-aware/more observant than you." Now you're just being "that guy." That guy needs his behind kicked. Don't be that guy. The purpose of your study is to understand and love your wife better. The purpose is not to be that guy.

An interesting and unintended consequence followed my becoming a student of Amy's family. I began to see my own family's model of doing family more clearly. I began to see the ways in which my upbringing impacted me – both for good and for not so good. It has, I hope, made me a better brother-in-law and son-in-law. When we welcomed my newest brother-in-law into the family, Tim and I were able to sit down and identify some uniquely McClellan characteristics. Again, some are good, some are notsomuch – but I was glad to be able to help him gain his bearings as the newcomer in a large extended family. I've also been able to appreciate Amy's family in ways I had never been able to do before. My in-laws love Jesus, they love their girls, they are terrific grandparents, and in spite of myself, they love me too. We've been blessed with wonderful, imperfect, loving, train-wrecks of families!

Reprioritizing Your Vocational Calling(s)
There is another way our family differences showed up in an unhelpful way. Amy's dad worked at the U.S. Post Office for much of his career. He had set work hours. He came home at the same time every day, and it would appear, he could leave work at work. He came home, changed his clothes, and was fully engaged on the home front. There weren't calls at all hours with

distraught folks needing his attention. This was the work model Amy and her sisters grew up with.

My dad was a teacher and coach who changed vocations when I was in the seventh grade. My dad has spent the last thirty years of his life as a beef feedlot nutritional consultant. Most weeks, he left on Monday mornings and got home on Friday nights. My dad is now in his sixties, and he still drives 60,000 miles a year to see his clients! He had a home office, and it was not unusual for dad to get phone calls at all hours. Unplugging was a conscious effort my father had to make, and we grew up with this work model as the norm.

Early in our marriage, this was a constant source of strife. The models were too different. I thought working all the time was just what men did, and ministry is very fertile ground for working all the time. The boundaries are blurry. Ministers have to be intentional about bringing balance to their home and vocational lives. Most of us do it poorly. Amy was frustrated that I worked "all the time." I was frustrated that she could not understand that this is what men do to take care of business and provide for their families. Why could she not understand that I have people who are depending on me to provide for them? I have to roll up my sleeves and go to work! This is what my dad did, because it's what men who love their families do. I heard her frustration as being a direct assault on my model of manhood. It wasn't, but that's how I received it given our very different models.

What was going on in our family was a reflection, not just of different family models and expectations, but also of the differences between men and women. Men, generally speaking, define themselves in terms of their work. Women, generally speaking, define themselves relationally. Watch an episode of "Wheel of Fortune" and pay attention to how the contestants introduce themselves. The men will always start with their vocation, even if they're unemployed or retired. The women start with their family: husband/kids/grandkids. We're wired differently.

This is not the result of some sort of evolutionary process. Rather, it reflects God's intention in creating us male and female. Justin Buzzard helpfully puts it this way, "Before God gave the first man a wife, he gave him a job.[1]" Our vocational calling as men consists of a twin command: work and keep (Gen. 2:15). Buzzard suggests that those words are better translated "cultivate and guard."[2] Herein lies the heart of a man's vocational calling. We are to cultivate and guard that which God has given us.

There are an infinite number of ways that this can be applied, but for our purpose one will suffice. I must cultivate and guard my family: my wife first and foremost, and my children secondarily. The Bible reminds us that this is indeed the proper order. We are not free to reprioritize our lives as we see fit. We cannot put the work of ministry in the first slot, and then leave our families to fend for themselves with the scraps of our guarding and cultivating.

---

1   Justin Buzzard, *Date Your Wife* (Wheaton, IL: Crossway, 2012), p. 41.

2   ibid.

This realization was both humbling and freeing. I can put the same amount of sweat and effort into my primary callings as a husband and father as I do in my tertiary calling as a pastor. That was the freeing part! My desire to work hard and get after it can find expression within the sphere of my family. The humbling part was that I had been doing nothing of the sort. While working is better than not working, pursuing one's work at the expense of your wife and kids is not an available option.

When things headed south in ministry, I felt lost. My vocation had been taken away from me. My fundamental identity as a dude was under serious assault. The first couple of months at Tates Creek were awful! I would sit and listen to my friend Mark Randle teach the Sunday School class we attended and I would think to myself, "This dude is a hack! He's likeable, and a great guy – but I could so teach this better than he is!" This was not helpful, and only served to fuel my lostness. My conversations with God went something like this, "How could you do this to me? You are subjecting these good people to listening to this guy, and I'm the one mule-ing porn at Amazon for ten hours at a pop?[3] How is this fair? How are you good?"[4]

---

3   Sadly, Amazon sells pornography. As a picker, you have no control over what kinds of materials you pull to ship. Ultimately, I left Amazon as a matter of conscience. Drug cartels use unwilling persons to transport drugs for them. These people are known as "mules." I was stuck "mule-ing" an equally destructive product – the only difference being the legality of the product.

4   While I know Mark has grown as a preacher and teacher, it was amazing how much better he got once I had repented and my attitude changed. In about a two-week time period, Mark went from a "no-talent hack" to a faithful and gifted teacher of God's Word. He remains a faithful and treasured friend.

Listening to John Sartelle was a great blessing. John is the most consistently excellent preacher I have ever heard. Some weeks may be better than others, but he was never unprepared in the pulpit. John preaches the gospel with a consistency I quickly realized I had never had. Then, one week, something happened. John was off his game. We were meeting weekly at that point in time, and so I brought it up during our time together. His reason shocked me. There was an issue in the life of one of his adult children that was causing him and his wife a great amount of emotional and spiritual duress. John didn't tell you his wife and kids came first; he modeled it for you. The ups and downs of vocational ministry did not knock him off his game. Trouble in his extended family did.

I wish I could tell you that the light bulb went on at that moment, and I got my act together immediately. Yeah, not so much. It did, however, prove a needed foundation for the work that has gone on and is ongoing in our marriage since we returned to Fremont. Our married life has not been easy. What it has always been is good. I now realize that my best work must be done in guarding and cultivating Amy and the kids.

One of my professors at Taylor, Mark Cosgrove, dedicated a book he wrote to his three sons, "In whose lives I must do my best writing." I can't even remember the title of the book, but the dedication stuck with me. My wife Amy, and our kids, Gabrielle and Nathaniel, deserve my "best writing."

They get my best more than they used to, but still not as much as they deserve. Old habits and models die slow and painful deaths.

That's the worst part of having a rough go in ministry, isn't it? It's our families who have to put up with us. The people we love the most are often the ones we treat the worst. While I don't have this one figured out, there is one final thing I do know: I've gotta work harder at family life than at ministry, and I'd be dead in the water if my wife and kids did not bestow grace upon me. If you've been a tool to your family, start by earnestly asking their forgiveness. By God's grace, you can rebuild from there. Become a student of your wife and her family of origin. They can't have been a total loss: they raised the woman you find more intriguing than any other person on the planet. Rework your vocational priorities. God will be honored, your family will reap the benefits, and ministry will seem less consuming when it's in the proper place. It's hard work, but that's what our Creator has wired us for!

Paul House did our pre-marital counseling. He told us in our first session that married life was all about receiving and bestowing grace on one another. His words have proven to be prophetic. There are plenty of days I don't want to treat Amy like she's a walking, talking exhibit of God's love for me. There are days I want, more than anything, to be "that guy" and recite the laundry list of ways I think her side of our family is unhelpful. There are days I want to throw myself into the vocation of being a pastor and totally neglect my family. Worse yet, there are days I actually do one or all of those things. I need my wife's forgiveness. I need her to be gracious. God, in His providence, has blessed me with such a wife.

I suspect you've been blessed in the same way. Let us thank God for it!

ENDING ON A GOOD NOTE

Two For the Road

The title *Mea Culpa* defines the previous chapters. There are, however, a couple of lessons I've learned that aren't negative and don't involve mistakes I've made. I share these here in the conclusion, largely because I'd like to end the book on a positive note. Wallowing in my own incompetence and sin has been a good, but uncomfortable, experience. Writing is a hard discipline, but the sense of my own awfulness has made a hard discipline almost impossible. For my own catharsis, I offer you "Two For the Road."

It's Not Always You
Now granted, it usually is you. That's the theme of the book, and really it's all you can control. You. Waking up for the third time without

a place of ministry brought about some serious soul-searching, and not just about me. I realized that my context needed to change. There was something about me and the way I'm wired, and the denominational situation in which I was laboring, that simply did not click. I'm not blaming the denomination. We simply were not a good fit. I had nonsense I needed to sort out, but I also needed to change my context.

When some of my Baptist friends wonder how I turned to "the dark side" of covenant baptism, they're missing part of the point. While my thinking on the nature of baptism has changed, it's the ecclesiology of the PCA that is most appealing to me. I am accountable to the other elders in my presbytery. There is mutual support and encouragement to be had. I cannot change my place of ministry without the approval of the presbytery. This is good news to me. When a situation gets so bad that the pastor is ready to resign, it's rarely a one-sided problem. Who will have the necessary "adult conversations" with all involved? Congregational polity has no good answer to that question. The Presbyterian answer is not perfect, but it's an answer I can live with. I can see my way clear to serious biblical ministry with this polity structure in place.

Please do not misunderstand me: no denomination is perfect. Every denomination has its nonsense. In my former denomination, there are arguments over whether or not the "Sinner's Prayer" is an acceptable evangelistic practice. In my current denomination, we spend three hours debating whether or not intinction is a valid way to observe the Lord's Supper.[1] Here's what I've learned. I like the new nonsense better. It's stuff I can, and am willing to tolerate. The other stuff made me nuts, and the polity offered me little cover as a minister trying to bring about biblical reform in a local church.

It may not be you. You may need to look around the evangelical landscape. This is not because you're right and they're wrong; you may just need a different set of nonsense to deal with. I'm not saying that you should compromise your basic theological convictions, but I am saying that you may need to be open to rethinking your denominational home. Thankfully I had good, faithful friends to help me navigate this decision. This brings me to the second happy thought.

The Importance of Authentic Friendship in Ministry

> A friend loves at all times, and a brother is born
> for adversity. (Prov. 17:17)

I have an indifferent relationship with Southern Seminary.[2] There's a part of me that wants to hate

---

1   I had to look it up also. The question is this: can you dip the bread into the wine and thereby share a common cup? The debate was ugly and mean-spirited. Clearly not enough guys went to public schools where you would get physically assaulted for being a mean know-it-all. Some public school fisticuffs were clearly needed, but none were offered. I would have even settled for some soccer hooliganism, given the general absence of necks and traps in the room. Nothing.

2   The fact that I met and married my wife while at Southern trumps everything, but in a purely ministerial sense, I remain torn.

Southern's guts (if that were really possible). SBTS helped me be biblically and theologically sound, but did not do a good job of preparing me for local church work. Looking back, I now know such preparation was impossible given when I was at Southern. Dr. Mohler and the administration were in a battle to recover an orthodox, biblically faithful Christian confession. While I got a great education, it was poor in preparing students for local, parish ministry. I've also come to realize that this may be outside the scope of what one can realistically ask a seminary to do, but this is a deep wound that is keenly felt. I am also aware that if I had gone to another seminary, I would be wrestling with the same indifference. The problem was mainly with me, not with Southern.

I'm not terribly enthusiastic about seminary education in general. I don't like taking someone out of the place where they know others and are themselves known and then asking them to do theological work. As was discussed in chapter two, place matters. To make a bad situation worse, the proliferation of online degrees feels like a bad punch line. Incarnational teaching ministry is going the way of the dinosaur, it would seem. I could defend yanking someone out of their local context to go to school if there is a relational benefit to doing so. This conviction brings me full circle: perhaps the greatest lasting benefit of going to a residential seminary is the friendships you make while pursuing your M.Div. As Paul House says, "This presumes a high view of friendship, not a low view of theological education." Throughout ministry, these friends have told me I was acting like an idiot (when indeed I was), yet they still came to my defense when the fruits of my stupidity came to full bloom. These friends, despite all evidence to the contrary, never gave up on me. Furthermore, as men committed to faithful preaching and teaching of the Bible, we've been able to have prolonged, serious conversations for close to two decades. Sadly, there has been little serious theological reflection on the nature of friendship within evangelical circles.

At the end of the day, I know there are a group of men that I can call no matter what. They love Jesus, they love my family, and they love me. I don't have to sugar coat anything. They know all my garbage. I know theirs. They know my strengths and weaknesses. They know what makes me tick, both good and bad. I met the majority of these men while in seminary. This life-on-life interaction does not happen if you're doing your course work "virtually." The portability of the degree program seems like a poor trade if I have to sacrifice those kinds of friendships, and I'm not buying the argument that you don't have to. The fact that some of my friends minister incarnationally within the academy gives me reason to hope in the entire enterprise. The tension between place and higher education is not one that is easily reconciled, and is obviously beyond the scope of this project. What I can reconcile, however, is that the friendships cultivated while pursuing higher education have been a means of grace. God has used/uses/will use those friendships mightily, and I am grateful for them. I pray you've been blessed similarly. I cannot imagine ministry without this kind of friendship.

CONCLUSION

Preachers are notoriously bad at "landing the plane." We know we ought to, but we just can't! There's always too much to do, and too little time to prepare the sermon. Here's my final pass: I realize it's possible to read through this book and think, "His poor wife and kids – those poor people he pastors! That guy is an idiot! There is so much more to pastoral ministry."

I agree.

This book is not a list of all the lessons you ought to learn as a pastor. Each of us has a model of ministry from which we operate. That model will have strengths and weaknesses. Each of us is unique in our giftings. Each of us unique in our shortcomings. We all have lessons to learn. I don't know what yours are. I barely know my own.

This book is offered as a warning, and hopefully as a means of hope. You don't have to do what I've done. You can minister differently than I have – in fact, I pray that you do. Nonetheless, we serve a God who uses clay pots to proclaim His glorious gospel! Remembering which is the clay pot and which is the glorious object is half the battle. If this book helps you in that way, then *Soli Deo Gloria*!

ACKNOWLEDGEMENTS

Writing this book has been a difficult journey. Thankfully, it has not been a solo trip. Lyrical theology is a seemingly new thing: but our best poets/songwriters have always been confessional. To that end, and because I am a product of the 1980s, the "lyrical theology" of Johnny Cash, Bruce Springsteen, Gordon Sumner (Sting), Roland Orzabal and Kurt Smith (Tears for Fears) have been welcome writing companions. When I need a more Christ-centered confession, Sara Groves, Matthew Smith, and Crystal Davy are my "go-to's". The body of Christ has shown love and support for our family in this process in a number of ways. First, I appreciate the friendship and accountability of my fellow teaching elders within the Platte Valley Presbytery. I enjoy ministry and life together with them; particularly when we're wading through a mess. Second, the folks and session of Grace Church are a gracious gift of God. Their prayers and kind support mean more to their pastor than I suspect they know. Planting Grace Fremont has been a wonderful journey made with wonderful people. Finally, Matt Gary, Bill Sindelar and Scotty Brant are the best programmer/coach/training partner a competitive powerlifter could ask for. Your efforts, skill and friendship keep me (somewhat) balanced, sane and "Strong like bull."

Four friends have remained constant across multiple years and places of ministry: Paul House, C. Ben Mitchell, Gregory Alan Thornbury, and Richard Bailey. Their friendship and counsel have been a means of grace. As House says in his written works, "You do not make friends like this. God gives them to you." Several other friends contributed in practical ways to the writing process. All are faithful ministers laboring in local churches: Gene Sherman, Adam Neel, Mark Randle, and Jim Moore read and gave comments on the manuscript. Any remaining weakness or awfulness is mine; their efforts have made this a better work. I already blamed Croft, but it bears repeating. Brian loves and serves pastors well. My engagement in this difficult task was a small token of my respect and esteem for Brian and Practical Shepherding.

My wife Amy is an unending source of love and encouragement. Our beautiful daughter Gabrielle and witty son Nathaniel bring laughter and joy into my life in ways I can't fully articulate. They are God's good gifts. We have, as an immediate family, been the recipients of the love and care of a wonderful extended family. Grandparents, aunts and uncles, and cousins give our family a sense of place and belonging. The love of the Broquard, Clark, Deacon, McClellan, Meyer, and Scott families has been a constant through the ups and downs of a seemingly itinerant ministry.

During the writing of this book, our new church experienced the unthinkable. One of our own, a young man of sixteen, was killed in a car accident along with two of his friends. Jackson Blick was a young man of great promise. His death came as a complete shock to all of us. Jackson's parents are dear friends, and have been so for a long time. Both sets of Jackson's grandparents attend Grace Church, and our extended families are old friends. Seeing Jodi and Eric mourn well the death of their son has been one of the most profound pastoral experiences of my life. If this book seems "uneven" in tone and voice, it's probably because some of it was written before Jax's death and some after. Finding my voice as a writer and preacher in the midst of such trying times has been hard. He was a good friend to our son Nathaniel, so the grief has been intense in our home. Our friends lost a son, and our son lost a friend. Theirs is the far greater, but not more legitimate, grief.

Wendell Berry has written one of the best and most powerful passages regarding grief I've ever read. I can no longer read it aloud. It overwhelms me when I try to do so. One of Port William's (Berry's fictional town) most endearing figures is Mat Feltner. His son, Virgil, has been reported missing-in-action during the Battle of the Bulge. Mat and his wife Margaret have taken in Virgil's young wife Hannah, who is expecting the couple's first child. One night, Mat wanders the streets of the village of Port William and finds the town barber, Jayber Crow. Though it's late, Jayber's shop has stayed open and he's reading a book. The ensuing conversation is easily my favorite Berry passage, with Jayber Crow serving as the narrator of his own story:

> *And then after a pause, speaking on in the same dry, level voice as before, he told me why he had been up walking about so late. He had had a dream. In the dream he has seen Virgil as he had been when he was about five years old: a pretty little boy who hadn't yet thought of anything he would rather do than follow Mat around at his work. He looked as real, as much himself, as if the dream were not a dream. But in the dream Mat knew everything that was to come.*
>
> *He told me this in a voice as steady and even as if it were only another day's news, and then he said, "All I could do was hug him and cry."*
>
> *And then I could no longer sit in that tall chair. I had to come down. I came down, and went over and sat beside Mat.*
>
> *If he had cried, I would have. We both could have, but we didn't. We sat together for a long time and said not a word.*
>
> *After a while, though the grief did not go away from us, it grew quiet.*[1]

When I harbored dreams of an academic life, I told myself my first book would be dedicated to my wife. However, we both agree that this is more fitting: to Jodi and Eric Blick. May the gospel quiet your grief.

---

1   Wendell Berry, *Jayber Crow* (Washington, DC: Counterpoint. 2000), p. 149.

Also available from

Christian Focus ...

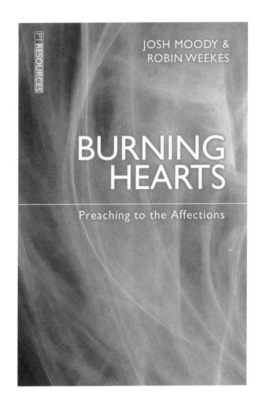

JOSH MOODY &
ROBIN WEEKES

PT RESOURCES

BURNING
HEARTS

Preaching to the Affections

ISBN 978-1-78191-403-8

Burning Hearts

Preaching to the Affections

JOSH MOODY & ROBIN WEEKES

Affection is often a neglected theme in our generation of Bible believing Christians. It has not always been so. Previous generations thought a great deal about the centrality of the heart in the Christian life and the need to preach to it. This book will prove a valuable resource as we learn about the place of the affections in our walk with Christ and in preaching Him to ourselves and others.

For some, this little book will be a healthy reminder; for others, it will revolutionize their preaching.

D. A. Carson
Trinity Evangelical Divinity School, Deerfield, Illinois

It has not only convinced me of the importance of preaching to the affections, but has also inspired me to think that I must and can do this better.

Vaughan Roberts
Rector of St Ebbe's, Oxford and Director of Proclamation Trust

Josh Moody is Senior Pastor of College Church in Wheaton, Illinois. His books include Journey to Joy,No Other Gospel,and The God-Centered Life. For more, visit www. GodCenteredLife.org.

Robin Weekes has pastored churches in Delhi, India and London, UK where he currently serves as the Minister of Emmanuel Church Wimbledon. He has also been involved with training Bible teachers both in North India and through being on the teaching staff of the PT Cornhill Training Course in London.

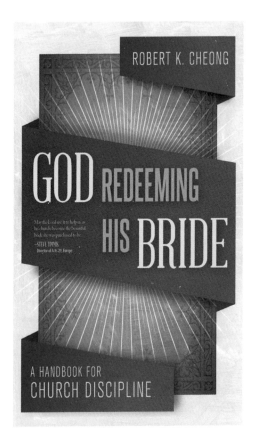

ROBERT K. CHEONG

GOD REDEEMING
HIS BRIDE

May the Lord use it to help us, as
his church become the beautiful
bride she was purchased to be.
—STEVE TIMMIS
Director of Acts 29, Europe

A HANDBOOK FOR
CHURCH DISCIPLINE

ISBN 978-1-84550-719-0

God Redeeming His Bride

A Handbook for Church Discipline

Robert K. Cheong

Church discipline is a term that is fraught with problems for the church today. However from the Biblical witness it is clear that it is an essential component of a healthy, God-honoring church - a church where Christians grow and mature in grace and develop solid foundations with which they can, with the help of the Spirit, withstand the storms of life.

With many years of pastoral experience, Robert K. Cheong has faced this issue many times. Additionally he interviewed over 30 pastors from different countries and a wide variety of church settings.

May the Lord use it to help us, as his church, become the beautiful bride she was purchased to be.

Steve Timmis
Executive Director of the Acts 29 Network & Pastor,
The Crowded House, Sheffield

A wonderfully practical and refreshingly gracious treatment of the topic. Even those who don't subscribe to everything Cheong says will find this book to be a significant help.

Thomas R. Schreiner
James Buchanan Harrison Professor of New Testament
Interpretation, The Southern Baptist Theological Seminary
Louisville, Kentucky

Robert K. Cheong is the pastor responsible for Care and Counselling at Sojourn Community Church, Louisville, Kentucky. He is married to Karen and they have three grown children.

Tim Cooper and Kelvin Gardiner

PASTORING
the PASTOR
Emails of a Journey through Ministry

"Convicting, compelling and ultimately uplifting"
Colin S. Smith

ISBN 978-1-84550-784-8

Pastoring the Pastor

Emails of a Journey through Ministry

TIM COOPER & KELVIN GARDINER

Daniel Donford is a new pastor: excited, filled with bright dreams, anticipating a big future for him and his new church. However opposition and obstacles lie just ahead, and both may end his journey into pastoral ministry before it has really begun. But Dan has an Uncle Eldon. The wisdom he offers, via a series of emails, might just be enough to see Dan transformed into the mature, selfless, loving pastor God wants him to be.

In this earthy and attractive page-turner of a book, we are exposed to the whole fascinating range of church Life and Christian ministry, joys, scandals and all.

Richard Bewes
Rector Emeritus of All Souls Church, Langham Place, London, OBE

Convicting, compelling and ultimately uplifting; this insightful probing of the realities of pastoral ministry will make you smile, lead you to pray, and encourage you to persevere.

Colin S. Smith
Senior Pastor, The Orchard Evangelical Free Church, Arlington, Illinois & President of Unlocking the Bible

Tim Cooper lives with his wife Kate and their four sons in Dunedin, New Zealand. He is Senior Lecturer in the History of Christianity in the Department of Theology and Religion at the University of Otago.

Kelvin Gardiner has pastored churches in New Zealand, the Philippines and the US. For ten years he led a ministry leadership organization overseeing one hundred US churches and providing pastoral support for overseas mission teams. He and his wife Jill currently offer pastoral care for mission agencies in Asia and Europe.

ALEC MOTYER

PREACHING?
Simple Teaching on Simply Preaching

"Alec Motyer has had a profound, formative influence on my preaching. In this book he puts his decades of wisdom on expository preaching at the reader's fingertips" Tim Keller

ISBN 978-1-78191-130-3

Preaching?

Simple Teaching on Simply Preaching

ALEC MOTYER

Like many things in life, the skill of good preaching is 95% perspiration and 5% inspiration. Alec Motyer's guide is based on a multitude of sermons over many years of preaching in many different situations, a recipe to help you know your subject and to pull the pieces together into a winning sermon. Preaching is a privilege: let Alec help you reach out and make the best of the gifts God has given you.

Alec Motyer has had a profound, formative influence on my preaching. In this book he puts his decades of wisdom on expository preaching at the reader's fingertips. This is as practical and Biblically solid a book on preaching as you can find today.

Tim Keller
Senior Pastor, Redeemer Presbyterian Church
New York City, New York

Alec's succinct and stirring treatise on preaching makes me wish wholeheartedly that I could start all over again-in that blessed privilege of preaching, praying and pastoring.

Dale Ralph Davis
Minister in Residence, First Presbyterian Church
Columbia, South Carolina

Dr Alec Motyer is a well-known Bible expositor and from an early age has had a love for studying God's Word. He was formerly principal of Trinity College, Bristol.

THE WORK
OF THE
PASTOR

WILLIAM STILL

"...a source of widespread inspiration and encouragement to several generations of younger ministers. May it continue to be that for the rising generation of pastors." **Sinclair B. Ferguson**

ISBN 978-1-84550-573-8

The Work of the Pastor

WILLIAM STILL

Gain an insight into the work of the pastor. It is based on the thesis that the pastor, being the shepherd of the flock, feeds the flock upon God's Word; the bulk of pastoral work is therefore through the ministry of the Word.

...plain, direct, filled with conviction, and soaked with pastoral observation and wisdom that nourishes the soul. The Work of the Pastor *has one main idea: Feed the sheep the Word of God. If you need encouragement to do that, or a vision for doing that, then read this book and be challenged.*

Thabiti Anyabwile
Assistant Pastor for church planting, Capitol Hill Baptist Church,
Washington, D.C.

The Work of the Pastor *is one of my favorite books to give away, and therefore I am delighted to see it back in print. William Still pastored the same city church for more than fifty years. By his absolute faithfulness to the Word of God and dedication to intercessory prayer, he became a leader for gospel renewal in the Church of Scotland. This small classic presents Mr Still's best thinking and most passionate convictions about the work of ministry that he loved so well and fulfilled so completely.*

Philip G. Ryken
President, Wheaton College, Wheaton, Illinois

William Still was minister of the Gilcomston Church of Scotland from 1945 until 1997. His ministry had a strong emphasis on Biblically based expository preaching.

Christian Focus Publications

Our mission statement –

STAYING FAITHFUL
In dependence upon God we seek to impact the world through literature faithful to His infallible Word, the Bible. Our aim is to ensure that the Lord Jesus Christ is presented as the only hope to obtain forgiveness of sin, live a useful life and look forward to heaven with Him.

Our books are published in four imprints:

CHRISTIAN
FOCUS

CHRISTIAN
HERITAGE

Popular works including biographies, commentaries, basic doctrine and Christian living.

Books representing some of the best material from the rich heritage of the church.

MENTOR

CF4•K

Books written at a level suitable for Bible College and seminary students, pastors, and other serious readers. The imprint includes commentaries, doctrinal studies, examination of current issues and church history.

Children's books for quality Bible teaching and for all age groups: Sunday school curriculum, puzzle and activity books; personal and family devotional titles, biographies and inspirational stories – because you are never too young to know Jesus!

Christian Focus Publications Ltd,
Geanies House, Fearn, Ross-shire,
IV20 1TW, Scotland, United Kingdom.
www.christianfocus.com